MAN

on the

THRONE

MAN

on the

THRONE

*Becoming the Spiritual Leader of Your Kingdom
within the Kingdom of God*

Jordan Burgen

For information contact :
Flatirons Community Church
400 W South Boulder Road STE 1700
Lafayette, Colorado 80026
flatironschurch.com

Book and Cover design by Jordan Burgen
Crown by Alvaro Cabrera from the Noun Project

ISBN: 978-1-54-399804-7
eBook ISBN: 978-1-54-399805-4

First Printing: January 2020

10 9 8 7 6 5 4 3 2 1

Dedicated To Leah, Jonah, Carter, and Eden

CONTENTS

FOREWORD

BY JIM BURGEN

ONE OF MY DUTIES AS A PASTOR is to perform wedding ceremonies. The usual protocol prior to the wedding day is for the couple to attend a premarital workshop and then, a few days before the ceremony, meet with me to work out the logistics of the ceremony.

I didn't know the young couple very well but I accepted the invitation when the prospective groom took me aside and said that while he didn't have the funds to pay the normal stipend for me to officiate, but instead, he did have a slightly used .45 caliber Sig Sauer handgun with built-in red-dot sights that he hoped I would accept instead. Now, to be clear, I was about to waive the stipend aside, but I thought to myself, who was I to rob him of his blessing of giving this generous gift? (Don't judge me. I live in the wild, wild west.)

When the big day arrived and all the guests were seated, just before the groom and I took our places at the front, off the cuff, I asked him a simple question: "Are you ready to be a husband?"

Most of the color drained out of his face, and all he could mutter was a whispered, "huh?"

I could sense a panic attack on the way so I quickly asked, "Are you OK?"

He just looked me right in the eyes with one of those "save me, I'm drowning" looks and said, "Yeah, I guess I haven't really thought about it like that." Cue the music, here we go.

I wish that this story was an isolated incident, but unfortunately, it's not. While no man really knows or is fully prepared or aware of what it means to join themselves to another person in the holy covenant of marriage, the reality is that most of the attention surrounding "getting married" revolves around flowers, colors, groomsmen, tuxes, wedding venues, honeymoon destinations, and housing adjustments. Very little thought or conversation takes place around actually BEING married.

The young man in my story was just thinking, "I'm getting married and heading to Cancun for a week of guilt-free, (hopefully) mind-blowing sex". He hadn't thought about the thousands of days and weeks that would follow the honeymoon. He was ready to GET married. He hadn't given any or much thought to what it meant to BE married or STAY married ... for the rest of his life, 'til death do us part. He was going to do what most of us men do. Try to figure it out or make it up as we go. Not a good plan.

Men, as a gender, are notoriously bipolar. Not in the

medical or psychological diagnostic sense, but in the way that we tend to operate our lives, especially when it comes to masculinity, marriage, and parenting. We swing from "I've got this, I can do this by myself, I don't need any help" to "This is impossible, this can't be fixed, this isn't what I signed up for, I don't want to do this anymore, I quit."

And, somewhere in between, there is a moment that has been growing for quite some time, like a volcano about to erupt. Typically, we try to ignore it, deny it, or distract ourselves with toys, hobbies, or activities. Or, just do what I do: keep plowing ahead thinking that with enough effort, hard work, or dedication, we'll figure it out or it will go away or fix itself. But it won't. That moment is called "exhaustion."

Men get exhausted, not because they are bad, weak, or stupid. Men get exhausted because we are wired to fix things, build things, protect things, figure stuff out, and get things done. Exhaustion comes when we do all that we know to do, try all that we know to try, change everything that we know to change, and what we thought was supposed to work, doesn't. But, somebody, somewhere, somehow let us know that "real men" should know what to do so we just keep doing more stuff until eventually, inevitably, we wear out, give up, tap out, and quit. And in the process, we leave a wake of carnage behind us. Not because we're bad, weak, or stupid. We're just frustrated, scared, and exhausted.

Trust me. I know. I type these words fresh off of my six-month sabbatical. A sabbatical is a season of rest, recovery, reconnection and restoration so that a soul that has been running hard for a long time can rest and heal so that he or she can return to the battle.

I'm a good man, husband, father, pop-pop, pastor, and leader. I've been doing ministry for almost four decades and this year, my wife and I celebrated our 35th wedding anniversary. But I was exhausted. And in that exhaustion, I had tunnel vision, blind spots, and unintended sideways energy which had caused wounds and pain to the people that I love the most: my wife, my family, my friends, and my staff. As an act of love and grace, the leaders in my life gave me the gift of rest.

Not long into it, I had my first sabbatical counseling appointment. I actually said these words before I could stop myself, "I wish that I was strong enough and smart enough to not need anyone's help," and I knew that "anyone" included God.

Does that strike a chord with you? Say it out loud. "I wish I was strong enough not to need anyone to help me, even God." Sounds crazy, doesn't it? It may be the first time you've ever said it out loud, but I (we) sure do live my (our) life like I'm (we're) trying to live that way. After all...

What kind of man can't figure out how to be a good husband?

What kind of man doesn't know how to be a great father?

What kind of man has to stop and ask for help or direction?

A weak man. A stupid man. A man who is not enough. A typical man. Which is why none of us have a tough time building a list of broken marriages, families, friendships, and relationships caused in part or in full, by angry, frustrated, scared, worn out, or passive men, all fueled by exhaustion. Something needs to change.

I recently read some of the writings of an old Quaker pastor named Thomas Kelly who penned these thoughts; "God is always the initiator. Even when we think that we have an idea or a plan, really, God is initiating something in our lives and we are responding either poorly or properly."

I think that my sabbatical was God's idea. My leaders administered it. At first, I fought it. I didn't want to "need it." But, as an act of love and grace, God initiated it because he wanted something good for me and I wasn't going to get there by myself.

Which brings me to this book that you hold in your hands. It's not just a Bible study, although its wisdom comes straight from God's Word. It's not a "how to" instructional manual. It's not a checklist for Biblical manhood, marriage, and fatherhood or 5 steps to becoming a great anything. Then, what is it?

What if you hold in your hands, a "God-initiated act of love and grace"? What if there really is a God who has a plan for your life and wants to give you an abundant life, first as a God-imaging man, then as a Christ-modeling husband and father?

What if God initiated and manipulated the universe so that you could hold in your hand, at this moment, a story of the journey of imperfect men being redeemed out of and above their circumstances, caused by their own mistakes or the mistakes of others, and being used to bring about the salvation of their families? And, what if, no matter where you are on your journey, no matter what kind of family you came from or find yourself in right now, what if God has a plan to redeem your past, present, and future so that those who love and need you most, will look at you and call you "blessed"? I truly believe that it's not a matter of "what if?" I believe it's true. It is true because God is a good father, YOUR father, and he wants good for you and those that He has entrusted to you.

I love what you're about to read on the pages of this book. I say that not because it is written by my son, Jordan. I say that because, at 57 years old, after doing ministry and marriage for 35 years, as I read and meditated on the truths that you are about to encounter, I experienced new grace. I experienced new hope. I met a new face of Jesus, the "husband," described to me, not by a grisly old seminary professor or condescending preacher, but by a young husband, father, and pastor who is currently on the front lines fighting the fight, not trying to remember how it used to be from a rocking chair on a front porch.

It was written by my son, but today, my son became my teacher. Thank you, Jordan, for this God-initiated gift of grace to, not just me, but to every man who reads it and to the wives and children who will be blessed because of what God taught them through you. God is a good Father. Christ is a good husband. So are you.

-Jim Burgen

Husbands, love your wives, as Christ loved the church and gave himself up for her.

Ephesians 5:25

CHAPTER 1
Where To Begin?

IF YOU WERE TO COME OVER TO MY HOUSE and take a look at the books on my bookshelves, you would almost immediately notice a theme. That is because I exclusively shop for books in one section of the bookstore: Fantasy/Sci-fi. And in this particular section, I tend to be blind to anything with spaceships on it and focus primarily on any books with dragons, knights, and swords on the cover. I am a total fantasy nerd. And I am proud of that fact. I read everything from C.S. Lewis and J.R.R. Tolkien to J.K. Rowling and George R. R. Martin. If the author's name has more than one initial in it, sign me up. I'll probably love it.

What I have found as I have read all these stories, and probably what drew me to them as a kid when I first fell in love with the genre, is that most of them have a similar theme. They usually revolve around a character who is completely unqualified and seemingly insignificant being thrust into a circumstance where a lot more is expected of them than they think they can handle.

Frodo was a tiny hobbit. Harry Potter was a neglected child living in a closet. Jon Snow was a lord's illegitimate son living in the shadow of his legitimate half-brothers. However, they all went on to do incredible things in their respective stories.

Well ... guess what? You have just been or are about to be thrust into a circumstance where a lot more is expected of you than you think you can handle. And I hate to say it but you are probably right. From your perspective right now, there is no way you can accomplish what needs to be accomplished. You are Frodo setting off for Mordor *alone*. You are Harry entering into the final battle with Lord Voldemort *without* ever going to Hogwarts. You are Jon Snow ... sorry my "nerdery" is getting out of hand. But you get the point. None of these characters *actually* remained unqualified. Someone always accompanied them or trained them for what was going to be expected of them down the road.

You would be foolish to enter into (or continue in) this insurmountable feat without becoming adequately equipped.

I don't think I am being at all dramatic when I say that this quest we have to go on as men is any less daunting than the quests of the most famous fantasy characters of all time. The lives and souls of our loved ones are at stake. Real enemies, be it Satan, culture at large, or someone else, are trying to kill and defeat them and us. A DARK WIZARD WITH A LEGENDARY WAND IS AT OUR ... sorry, there I go again.

What I am *trying* to say is that marriage is HARD! Fatherhood is HARD! So come with me as I lead you on this magical journey of adventure and peril as we try to figure out what it looks like to successfully be the spiritual leader of your home!

WHAT DOES "SPIRITUALLY LEADING YOUR HOME" MEAN?

This is a question I have consistently struggled with. When I think of the role of a husband and father, the words "provide" and "protect" always come to mind. I must provide – put food on the table, make sure there is a roof over their heads, and make sure everyone has clothes that, for the most part, fit – and I must protect – make sure everyone in my house is as safe as I can possibly make them from threats, both foreign and domestic, or something like that. But is that it? I've always heard this other phrase– "spiritual leader of the home" – floating around out there. When *that* comes to mind, the real fear starts to sink in. "Provide and protect" is tangible. Results can be seen immediately. But how do I *lead* them, especially in spirituality? What is expected of me? What "counts"?

I think the best place to start when trying to tackle this question is figuring out what the Bible means when it lays out its instructions. It gives a lot of guidelines to the roles and relationships between a father/husband and his family, but it by no means spells it out in great detail. There is no book of the Bible dedicated to the detailed situations a husband/father finds himself in and how to deal with each one. Nor is there one with a checklist of everything you should do with your family to make them more spiritual. So, what is it talking about exactly when it says, "Love your wife"? That is vague.

I think this is why so many young men heading into marriage do not know exactly what they are getting into. They don't know what is expected of them because they assume they know what "love your wife" means, but fail to grasp the big picture. And, I believe, this starts with a failure to grasp what marriage actually is. So, the first question we must answer is: what is marriage?

At its core, marriage is a representation of the relationship between Christ and His Church. Paul states this very clearly in Ephesians:

> "Therefore a man shall leave his father and mother and hold fast to his wife, and the two shall become one flesh." This mystery is profound, and I am saying that it refers to Christ and the church. (Ephesians 5:31-32)

Just before this, in verse 25, he states, "Husbands, love your wives, as Christ loved the church and gave himself up for her ... "

Another term for this spiritual leading of the home, which you may have heard before, is Biblical male "headship." This is a term fraught with controversy in today's culture, but all it really means is that the Bible calls the male in the marriage to carry the responsibility of being the head or leader of the household. Ephesians 5:23 says this: "For the husband is the head of the wife even as Christ is the head of the church, his body, and is himself its Savior." *So, in trying to understand what it means to lead your home, we must first understand how Christ leads the Church.*

At the forefront of everyone's mind, especially since it is

directly stated in verse 25 we just saw, is that He "gave himself up for her." He literally died for the Church. And if it comes to that in your marriage, where you must choose between your life or hers, or that of your sons or daughters, you are called to do the same. I have never met a man who would say he would not die for his family. It is easy to grasp and a very noble promise. But it is usually theoretical. Most men don't have to do that for their family. It does demonstrate the extreme of how our love should be shown, but how are we supposed to love and lead when their lives aren't on the line?

Luckily, that isn't the only thing Scripture tells us Christ did for the Church, so there are plenty of other applications. Here is a list of some of the other ways that Christ led and loved the Church, especially in regard to spiritual leadership. We will dive into each of these later:

- He knew His role and who sent Him, and prepared accordingly
- He dealt with obstacles to His and the Church's success (Temptation, Pharisees, and Fear)
- He lived and led out of the blessings God had given Him
- He taught, prayed, and worshiped with His people
- He attended to His own spirituality and relationship with the Father
- He commissioned them to continue the work of the Father
- He gave them good gifts (Grace and the Holy Spirit)

- And all of these were done for the glory of God, not to glorify Himself or his Church

So, again, what does "spiritually leading your home" mean? It means all of those things. None can be left out. Each is a brick in the structure of a spiritually healthy home, which stands firmly on the foundation: Christ. What I will try to explain in these pages is how to use those bricks to successfully build your home.

WHAT MARRIAGE IS *NOT*

Here I would like to take some time to discuss what marriage is *not*. First of all, though marriage is a representation of the relationship between Christ and the church, it is *not* an exact replica. There are some very clear differences.

You are a man. A fallen man. You are not your family's Savior or Messiah. You are absolutely not their God, and any attempt to assume those roles is wrong. Those roles belong to Jesus. And though this may seem easy to understand, myself and many other men have fallen into the illusion that a wife's submission to her husband is absolute. Whatever we say goes, and however we do things is above reproach. Here is some hard truth: you won't be getting sex anytime you want it. Food won't be hot and ready for you every evening when you get home from work. Your wife is not you servant who is at your every beck and call. This is a false assumption and based on the (sometimes) unconscious conclusion that we are the absolute king of our house. But we're not. Christ is King.

Of you and everybody in your household. You and your family answer to Him. They first submit to Him, and then submit to you if you're spiritually worth submitting to. Their submission to you is an act of obedience to God and how He has designed the family unit to operate.

In the book of Hosea, who was a prophet (someone who directly heard from God and communicated what He said to the people of Israel), God says this:

> "And in that day, declares the LORD, you will
> call me 'My Husband,' and no longer will you
> call me 'My Baal.'" (Hosea 2:16)

This word translated here as "My Baal" is the Hebrew word for "master" and is translated as such in other versions of the Bible, like the NLT. This word carried the connotation of someone powering up over weaker people and ruling them in an unloving way with an iron fist. In this prophecy, God is telling the people how He intends to lead the church through Christ in the future: by being their "husband" and not their "master."

The role we have as husbands and fathers can be very rewarding. However, it is not a license to act and treat our families however we want. It is a heavy responsibility. We have been called and placed by God to lead our families in the way *He* wants them to be led.

Another good way to understand what marriage is not is by looking at what Christ *didn't* do for the Church, or perhaps didn't do to the church. He never forced the Church to do anything. He offered Grace and we either accept it or we don't. He never withheld provision or protection. He was never hateful; everything He did was in love. And perhaps most profound in regard to marriage, is that He never *charged* us for anything. We never had to earn His love or grace. He gave it freely.

The role of the husband/father is active, not passive. The guidelines for that role are imperatives of what *we* are to do for our families (lead, provide, protect, serve), not what they should be doing for us. Similarly, we should not act out our role as husband and father only if the ones we lead are pulling their weight. As Paul would write, "*While we were still sinners, Christ died for us*" (Romans 5:8), and you are the head of your family whether they are acting as they "should" or not. Your role and the fulfillment of that role should be your main priority. Their roles are their responsibility.

Can you offer instruction and guidance to a disrespectful wife or a disobedient child? Of course! As long as it is done the way Jesus did it: in love.

When I say "in love," all I mean by that is in a way, that in the long run, will bring you closer together. Anything that drives a wedge in a relationship with the ones that are closest to you is probably not loving. For example, say you have an agreement with your wife to never criticize or correct each other harshly in front of the kids, so as to maintain a united front in parenting. However, you end up saying something to one of the kids that rubs her the wrong way and she, in full view of everyone in the house, makes it known that you screwed up and she is mad. The kids may now be thinking that as well, and may be starting to get mad at you simply because mom is. You now have a few options as to how to handle this. First, you could make her feel as bad as you feel now by biting back and putting her down in front of everyone. Or second, and this is probably counterintuitive, you could stick to the original agreement, pull her aside in private, and address the issues there – both the original issue she was upset about and the issue of her breaking the "unified front" agreement.

Your initial "want" in responding to her may be to make her feel bad, but if you step back and look at the greater "want" in your relationship, it is probably to be as close to your wife as possible. Open, contentious conflict is probably not the best way to grow closer to her. Sticking to agreements, building trust, and showing her that you can deal with conflict in a mature, loving manner is a much better way.

You may be asking yourself now: "Why are gender roles so important in all of this, anyways? Isn't that just an outdated way of looking at relationships?" It is important because God set it up that way from the beginning for a very specific purpose. God created mankind in His image (in the Hebrew, this is a masculine noun) and His likeness (feminine). Hebrew nouns were assigned a "gender," much like Spanish nouns are. It doesn't mean they have anything to do with human genders; it is more of a way to classify them for whatever reason. But the designation does draw some interesting parallels. When a male and a female come together in marriage, along with God, they create a union that is a representation of the Holy Trinity. Each part has its role, and when we start to mess around with those roles, we mess around with the representation as well, making it into something God never had in mind. (This is also why God hates divorce: divorce separates this "trinity" and destroys the picture of intimacy that God wishes to have with us.) I'm not saying that only men have the "image" and only women have the "likeness" and we are only completely revealing God if we are married. Both genders have the full image and likeness of God in them and no human makes us "complete" aside from Jesus. However, if we could each view our gender and the gender of our wives within this paradigm, we actually *elevate* the importance of marriage, family, and even sex. They become something worth protecting and prioritizing (as opposed to just arbitrary rules to follow).

One final note before we move on is this: everything you do as a husband and a father should be to glorify God, not yourself. You are out of line and have lost sight of your role if you are, at any point, trying to glorify yourself. This is the reason for our existence, and marriage and fatherhood are no exception.

YOUR KINGDOM

Another way to look at the relationship between you and your family is in the sense of a "kingdom." Though you are not a "king" in the dictatorial sense of the word, you have been given leadership, authority, and influence over everything that God has entrusted to you. But kingdoms do not run themselves. There is a certain way that a kingdom must be established and structured so that it is successful and glorifying to God.

The best picture I have found in Scripture of a kingdom that was established and structured the right way (at least for a while) is the kingdom of Solomon. King Solomon was the wealthiest, most influential, most successful, and wisest king (next to Jesus) to ever walk the earth. So, I think it is safe to say he had some measure of success. And while his kingdom stretched far beyond the bounds of his immediate family, there are some very important parallels that we can take wisdom from:

1. He had a plan. There was no doubt in his mind that He was to be the king of Israel after his father's death. Solomon was chosen by God to be David's successor. (And then after being declared the successor, David gave him some very wise advice and instruction.) *1 Kings 1:28-2:9*

2. After becoming king, he followed that advice and removed all of the obstacles to having a successful kingdom. In doing so, he purged the sin that could have meant his immediate downfall. *1 Kings 2:13-46*

3. Once the administration was purged, God offered him a blessing of his choosing. Solomon chose wisdom, and it was bestowed on him, as well as everything he could have chosen instead. *1 Kings 3:1-15*

4. After receiving that blessing, he lived and ruled out of it. He used his God-given wisdom to speak into the lives of the people he was leading. People from all over the world came to him to seek his wisdom. *1 Kings 3:16-4:34*

5. He established customs of worship in his kingdom. He built a temple for the Lord and led regular sacrifices and prayer. He was the driving force of these spiritual disciplines, ensuring that his kingdom would glorify God and grow in Him. *1 Kings 6, 8, 9:25* Similarly, he built massive amounts of infrastructure with the wealth God had given him, with the sole purpose of glorifying God. *1 Kings 6-7*

6. However, towards the end of his rule, not everything was positive. Solomon turned from the Lord, lured away by lust and false gods. And who paid the consequences for this? You think it would have been Solomon, but it wasn't. The kingdom remained with Solomon until his death. Instead, God took it away from his son, Rehoboam. The fallout of our actions always lands on the ones closest to us. *1 Kings 9:1-9; 11:1-43*

In the following chapters, we will dive into each of these areas. We will also look at the parallel of Solomon's reign with the way Christ led and loved the Church. And we'll discover what any of this has to do with spiritual leadership in the home.

This mystery is profound, and I am saying that it refers to Christ and the church.

Ephesians 5:32

CHAPTER 2
Mission & Calling

1 Kings 1:28-2:9
Deuteronomy 6:4-9, 20-25
John 17

CLARIFYING SOME TERMS

BEFORE WE GET ROLLING, I WANT TO MAKE sure we are all on the same page as far as terms. I will be using the terms "mission," "calling," and "purpose" a lot throughout this book and especially in this chapter. They are used interchangeably. There are also two distinct missions I will refer to in your life. The first is your overall mission in life. This is what you are called by God to do on this earth, your purpose for living, what gives you life, what fills your spiritual tank, and gives you a sense of meaning. Unfortunately, a lot of people don't know what theirs is. They either diminish their calling to whatever their job is at the time, or just go about life aimlessly. As men, many of us think that our purpose is to just make enough money to not feel like a failure.

I could probably write an entire other book about this topic alone, but I just want to note a couple of things about a man's general mission in life before we move on to get you thinking about what yours may be if you don't already know, because at least having an idea about this one is important before we get into the next one.

First, our God-given missions in life usually address what we see wrong in the world. It is something you have a legitimate passion for fixing. The reason for this is profound. Usually what we see wrong in the world has something to do with how we were wronged earlier in life. Our wounds in childhood, especially, shape our lives as we grow up. There are generally two things we do with those wounds. We let them control us or we address the issue and try to change things. When we address these wounds and go about trying to change things, a mission in life is born. This is one way God can redeem our painful pasts for good.

Second, your mission in life can be applied to whatever circumstances you are in at any given time. The career you pick will probably line up fairly close with your mission (if you know what that is) and if they don't, you are probably miserable. Our missions can be applied within the context of our relationships. Missions are rarely so specific that only one career or situation can help us to fulfill it.

Third, if you are a Christian, your mission should line up with God's overall mission of establishing His Kingdom on earth, meaning that it should line up with your God-given gifting and talents, and what you see wrong in the world is something that God sees wrong in the world.

For example, maybe you grew up in a poor family and never had the necessities in life that other people did. This left you with a wound of never being enough, never feeling safe, and perhaps a sense of injustice against you. You have two choices here: you can either succumb to these feelings and live your life as someone who will never amount to much and relies on other people for every need in life, or you develop a sense of purpose to right this wrong and it becomes your mission to attack poverty and injustice in the world. This is a great mission that is fueled by a specific wound and can be applied in many ways. For example, this could be applied by taking responsibility for your life and becoming a generous giver who tries to help others out of poverty. Or it could take the shape of making a caeer out of attacking world hunger on a global scale.

So, if you have not figured out what your overall mission in life is, take some time to contemplate this. You don't have to have it all figured out before you move on, but it will be helpful to know *something*. (On the next page is a quick journaling worksheet to get you thinking about this and hopefully narrow down some options for you. It is not meant to be all you need to identify your mission, just a little jump start.)

However, every man who is or wishes to be a husband and father has an additional, specific mission: *Be the spiritual leader of your home.* This is what the main portion of this chapter will explore.

The main point of this is that whatever your mission in life is, if you choose to lead a family as well, the mission of spiritual leadership of that family is added on. Take the example from above. If your mission in life is to attack poverty and injustice, great. But if you want to do that and also have a wife and kids,

MISSION WORKSHEET

1. What is the main problem you see in the world that you would change if you could? *(e.g., drug addiction)*

2. Look "upstream" from this problem. Is there something in the world, some underlying societal or moral issue, that is causing this problem at a deeper level? *(e.g., fatherlessness)*

3. Can you remember a time in your life when this same societal or moral issue was impacting your life in a very personal way? *(e.g., didn't have a dad)*

4. When this was happening, what did you really want? *(e.g., love, affirmation, and relationship)*

5. What are you really good, gifted in, or just love doing? *(e.g., hunting)*

6. How can you use your gifiting and passions to impact the problem you see in the world? *(e.g., take at-risk, fatherless kids hunting)*

you cannot neglect them to focus solely on feeding the poor (1 Timothy 5:8).

So what is the mission of a spiritual leader of the home? I'm glad you asked. Let's begin.

REGARDLESS OF YOUR MISSION, THIS IS YOUR MISSION.

The mission of the leader of the family is made very clear in Deuteronomy:

> "Hear, O Israel: The LORD our God, the LORD is one. You shall love the LORD your God with all your heart and with all your soul and with all your might. And these words that I command you today shall be on your heart. You shall teach them diligently to your children, and shall talk of them when you sit in your house, and when you walk by the way, and when you lie down, and when you rise. You shall bind them as a sign on your hand, and they shall be as frontlets between your eyes. You shall write them on the doorposts of your house and on your gates." (Deuteronomy 6:4-9)

As husbands and fathers, we are the ones with the responsibility to first love God with all of our "heart, soul, and might," and then to teach our families about who God is and how we are to love Him. This is a huge responsibility. To some it may seem impossible. After all, most of us are not pastors with an M.Div. or a PhD in Biblical Studies. But according to the Bible, that is no excuse to not meet this responsibility. A few verses later, it lays it out rather specifically. It says that your son will come to you with questions about God and what his commandments mean. And when he does, it is your responsibility to answer those questions, or at least go and find the answers. You may feel unqualified, and you might be. But knowing your calling is the *first step*, though not the last, into successfully acting it out.

Solomon's call on his life was clear as well, though just as insurmountable as ours may seem. He was selected by God and his father to be the next king of Israel. And furthermore, at least on paper, *he was unqualified!* He was not the oldest living son of David; Adonijah was. By all rights, the kingdom should have been Adonijah's. But God qualified Solomon instead. He provided what was needed for Solomon to live out his calling. And what was needed was an official declaration that Solomon would be king after David's death, which David gladly produced, much to the dismay of Adonijah.

God will provide you with the necessary tools to complete the tasks he has given to you. 2 Peter 1:3 says, "His divine power has granted to us all things that pertain to life and godliness, through the knowledge of him who called us to his own glory and excellence..." But that does not mean that we should just sit idly by, hoping that when those questions come we will magically have an answer pop into our heads.

The questions will come, from our sons as well as our wives and daughters, so we must begin to prepare now for them! The first step may be just *knowing* and *accepting* your calling, but the second is *preparing* to act it out. God has provided us with His Word and commanded us to study it. Getting a firm grasp on Scripture and a sound Biblical worldview is essential in spiritually leading your kingdom.

Solomon did this by listening to and following the words of his father, David. In one of my favorite passages of Scripture, David lays out exactly how Solomon should lead his kingdom:

> When David's time to die drew near, he commanded Solomon his son, saying, "I am about to go the way of all the earth. Be strong, and show yourself a man, and keep the charge of the Lord your God, walking in his ways and keeping his statutes, his commandments, his rules, and his testimonies, as it is written in the Law of Moses, that you may prosper in all that you do and wherever you turn, that the Lord may establish his word that he spoke concerning me, saying, 'If your sons pay close attention to their way, to walk before me in faithfulness with all their heart and with all their soul, you shall not lack a man on the throne of Israel.'
> (1 Kings 2:1-4)

I love those words: "Be strong, and show yourself a

man." Those are strong words! They are strong because it is a command, not a suggestion. In addition, he equates this manliness with following God because they are one and the same. And if Solomon does it right, "his word concerning" David, which was God's promise to David that Israel would "not lack a man on the throne," would be established. The reverse side of this coin, however, is that if Solomon does not follow God, Israel will lack a man on its throne. In the figurative sense, the person sitting on the throne wouldn't be a real man, if the above definition of manhood is true. In the literal sense, God would remove him and David's line would no longer rule Israel.

The same can be applied to our kingdoms as well. If we follow God and show ourselves men, then God will bless us and our families will thrive. But if we don't follow Him, not only will we suffer but our families will suffer and we will watch its members drift away, probably with some pretty deep father and/or husband wounds.

Another interesting point here is the Hebrew word that is translated as "man" in the above passage. The word is אִישׁ, pronounced "iysh." This word can be translated as "man" as it is here, but it can also be translated as "husband," and is throughout the Old Testament. This is the same word from Hosea 2:16, which we discussed in the previous chapter. God Himself refers to Himself as Israel's "אִישׁ" in Hosea 2:16. So, basically, David is telling Solomon to be the husband to his kingdom just as God is the husband to Israel, and likewise Christ is to the Church now.

Knowing your calling and what is expected of you is of vital importance. Too many men these days jump into marriage without knowing or contemplating the full weight of the mission, calling, and responsibility that they are promising their wife that they are ready and able to deliver. And because they are not prepared, their families do not thrive. Wives know when their husbands are weak. Children can sense when their dad is passive. This results in resentment and a leadership vacuum in the home. Many men lose their families outright because they did not show themselves men.

We've all seen this weakness play out: an overbearing wife who makes every decision because she is forced by her passive husband to step into that leadership void. Wild children and teenagers who don't have an ounce of respect for their parents. Fatherless households. Weak, passive husbands who forfeit the trust of their wives, leading to emotional or sexual affairs. Sexually immoral husbands who step outside of marriage to satiate their lustful appetites. While there is no excuse for a person to choose sin, these reasons certainly fuel the felt need to choose sins. And a lot of the times, these things could have been avoided if the man of the house had come in knowing his calling, what he was supposed to do, and did it.

How many more marriages could have been saved if young men knew what they were getting into? How many more children would have active, loving fathers in their lives if their dads knew their calling and were prepared for it?

Now, don't let this make you think that your other callings in life are now void. They aren't! God has gifted you in multiple ways to bring His Kingdom to earth. It's just that that if you decide you want to be a husband and father, which you are by no means required to do, this calling of being the spiritual leader of your home takes priority over every other mission that you might have, second only to your personal relationship with Christ. Paul even says in 1 Timothy 5:8 that the he who ignores this responsibility "has denied the faith and is worse than an unbeliever." It is not up for debate. It is that important. Your other mission cannot blot out this one. If God has truly called you to do both things, he will adequately *equip* you to do both things, as well as give you the grace and mercy you need when you fail. It is a huge task, and some men aren't up for it. That is perfectly fine if you haven't already entered into a marriage.

Also, it is important to note that it isn't always a matter of deciding if you are up for it or not. It's more than if you *want* to or not. Sometimes our God-given callings in life are strenuous and demand 100% of us all the time. No matter your calling, you should take a good long look at whether the calling of marriage is actually compatible with it. Sometimes, the answer is "no," or "not yet." That can be hard to swallow, especially in a Christian culture where marriage is sometimes expected of you. But accepting this can save you from years of frustration and hardship later. After all, it is better to be single and wish you were married than be married and wish you were single.

If the answer is "yes," then great! Just make sure that your future wife knows about it (your God-given calling in life) and is on board with supporting you in it. Make that a priority in finding a wife. That isn't a topic to bring up *after* the wedding.

So, we have established that knowing your calling is an essential first step to fulfilling that calling. And we have an even better example in Scripture than Solomon of someone knowing exactly what *His* calling was in regard to his relationship with the Church: Jesus.

JESUS KNEW HIS CALLING

Imagine if Jesus didn't know His calling when He came to earth. He would have probably continued in the trade of His father, Joseph, as a carpenter, and we might now have a few extra chairs in some museum of ancient Judea. But that's about it. His sermons that we find in the Gospels would have never shown people a better way to do life. He would have never challenged the graceless legalism of the Pharisees. And most importantly, He would have never died on a cross, paying for our sins with His blood.

Fortunately, Jesus *did* know His calling when He came to earth. Scripture is clear that from a young age He was in the temple, learning and astonishing people with his understanding and wisdom (Luke 2:41-52). Even though He was God in the flesh, he spent time preparing for the ministry He would implement in His later years. And when the time was *right*, He started that ministry at the age of 30.

I don't know why He didn't start earlier. Most people start their careers earlier than 30. But He chose to wait until the time was right. He didn't rush into it.

You've probably figured out where I'm going with this: *don't rush into marriage!* Starting such an endeavor before you are spiritually prepared can be detrimental to its success. I'm not saying wait until you are 30. The time wasn't "right" for Jesus because He was 30; the time was right because He was spiritually prepared.

With that said, you don't have to be a perfect man who has mastered everything before you are ready to be married. A lot of growing and refining happens within the context of marriage. There are many things that you just cannot know or learn until you are in the thick of it. All I mean by being prepared is that you should be aware of what you are getting into, and are taking steps to become the man your wife will need. She is counting on you and she is taking a risk putting herself under your leadership. She doesn't have to do that.

So, what kind of man did she choose? Is it one who will lead her, provide for her, and protect her and the family you create together like Jesus intended? There is no magic number that *needs* to be in your bank account first. You don't *have* to have a bachelor's or master's degree before you find a wife. You don't have to be able to write a dissertation on the female mind before your wedding day (it would be completely wrong, anyways). As in Genesis, your wife is given to you as a helper, and she will *help* you to become the man you want to be, and through your relationship, God will refine you into that man alongside your wife. All that to say: don't wait *too* long! You can learn and prepare yourself for some things, but a bunch of the learning happens *in* marriage.[1]

For example, there is an element of being single where it is natural to be selfish. Not necessarily in a prideful, egotistical way but there isn't anyone else you are constantly having to make sure is taken care of. Hence the word "single." You can do what you can to learn how to be more generous with your time and money, but at the end of the day, the responsibility to take care of others isn't necessarily the most important issue. You can spend your money how you want to. You can decorate your room, apartment, or house the way you want to. You can go to bed when you want to. You can clean up when you want to. Decisions in general are made on your own. However, when you get married, there is another person thrown into the mix that you are now "one" with. You are bound to her in everything. This is something you will never be able to adequately prepare for. Both of you will learn how to live in an entirely new way after the ceremony. You will learn how to make decisions together, both small and big. You will come to agreements on how best to order your day-to-day life. Your finances will no longer be just yours. And there are a thousand other things that you will never even have thought of that will spring up and need to be figured out. And just because there is a selfish tendency that marriage reveals in you doesn't mean that it is necessarily bad before you are married.

[1] I know I have now said in two different places to both "not rush into marriage" and at the same time "don't wait too long." There is somewhere between those two sentiments an amazing middle ground where you aren't still an immature boy but are not yet a man who has mastered masculinity and has no need of a wife. It can even be argued that a man without the "gift of celibacy" (which is a highly misjudged term) can't even reach true masculine responsibility without the help of a woman. For more on this read Douglas Wilson's Father Hunger, Chapter 9 [Nashville, TN: Thomas Nelson, 2012] and/or his blogpost about the subject: https://dougwils.com/s7-engaging-the-culture/7-reasons-young-men-marry-23rd-birthday.html

Being single allows you to be selfish a bit. But being married has its sacrifices and inherent responsibilities. It is, at its core, *selfless responsibility*. And that can only be learned when you are in the thick of it.

A small example for me was my overall lack of tidiness. I'm not a very organized person. If you could see my desk right now, you would undeniably agree. I was always the kid in school who just had papers jammed into his backpack with no regard for folders or binders. My dresser was a jumbled mess of unfolded clothes. My room in general was usually a disaster. As I got older, I found I functioned pretty well despite this. So, I never really saw the need to change much, which was my prerogative as a young, single man. However, once I got married, a few things obviously had to change. I had to learn that leaving laundry all over the apartment was not an acceptable decision. Dishes had to be done more regularly than once a month. The vacuum cleaner exists for a reason. Things like that. And while there are still areas that I (and my wife) allow to be messy, for the most part my organization and sense of responsibility for the things I own has greatly improved, thanks to the extremely gracious reminders from my wife.

But let's get back to the issue at hand: what was Jesus' calling and mission in life? Jesus states exactly this in the book of John:

> When Jesus had spoken these words, he lifted
> up his eyes to heaven, and said, "Father, the

hour has come; glorify your Son that the Son may glorify you, since you have given him authority over all flesh, to give eternal life to all whom you have given him. And this is eternal life, that they know you, the only true God, and Jesus Christ whom you have sent. I glorified you on earth, having accomplished the work that you gave me to do. And now, Father, glorify me in your own presence with the glory that I had with you before the world existed. (John 17:1-5)

His mission was to give eternal life to everyone God had entrusted to Him, so that God could be glorified. He goes on after this to be specific in the ways in which He provided this for His Church: things like teaching them the Word and guarding them from the evil one. He prays for them to be sanctified and to continue to be protected. And in saying that His time had come, He predicts the ultimate way He would provide this: His death.

The thing to note here that is important regarding knowing His calling, is in verse 4: "I glorified you on earth, having accomplished the work that you gave me to do." This implies that God gave Him work to do, and Jesus knew what it was. He knew His calling! And because He knew it, He was actually able to *do* it.

He also knew who sent Him. And that is key for us when entering a marriage. God has entrusted us with part of His kingdom, namely one of his daughters and perhaps one or more of His children. If we are to enter into a marriage, and eventually grow an entire family, then we must know that being a husband and father is the "work" that God has given us to do. And if God has given us this work, then we should not take it lightly and rush into things. Know what you are signing up for and prepare, and never quit preparing! Too much is at stake to start blindly!

WHAT IF YOU'RE ALREADY MARRIED?

As most of this book is directed at men who are not married yet, I want to address directly those reading who are already married and feel like they've already screwed up. First, let me say this: ME TOO! I was almost seven years into my marriage and almost five years into fatherhood when my wife sat me down and told me I was not being the spiritual leader of our home that she and my two sons needed. I didn't know exactly what I was getting into when I said, "I do." I will get into more of my story later, but I just want to let you know that it is not too late to steer the "ship" in a different direction.

There is never a better time to start being the spiritual leader of your home than right now. It may seem uncomfortable to you and foreign to your family, but they will begin to see your intentions and start to appreciate the new version of you, especially when they see and feel the benefits that come in their direction by your actions, not just your words. Figuring out what your calling is, even if you have already started, is still important. To use the ship metaphor, it may be ideal to know where you are going before you leave port, but if you find yourself wandering in the ocean and it is *there* that you receive your orders, you can change direction and still fulfill your duty.

There will be some challenges. Perhaps you have been going the wrong way for many years. Perhaps you have been anchored in a comfortable place for a long time. It may be hard to get the ship up and running again. Your family may be resistant to change. But that does not mean that you should not change course and from this point on begin to follow the mission that your commander has given you.

Now, don't bust into the house one day and declare, "Things are about to change around here!" Ships don't change course instantly. Some can take miles to get pointed in the right direction. Come at it with a servant's heart, in love, knowing that your family will need time to adjust. Stay true to the course and persevere. It won't happen all at once, but your family will thank you. Maybe not immediately. Actually, maybe never. Doesn't matter. Your mission is to steer that ship to port.

So, throughout this book, try and see how you can use these truths and apply them to your family now. Even men who start out on the right course will find themselves lost sometimes. You are not alone.

JACOB'S STORY

Jacob had been married for a couple of years when I met him. Those first couple years had not been easy at all for a couple of reasons.

First, his father had been a terrible leader of their home. Jacob grew up trying to prove to his dad that he was worthy of love through performance in sports and eventually his career. There had been no spiritual guidance or any sort of leadership outside of demanding perfection.

Second, a series of career setbacks, mostly due to the actions of other people, right at the start of Jacob's marriage left him feeling like a failure in life, mainly because of the perfection expectation he had carried his entire life. He didn't feel like he could provide for his new wife at all. This led to depression and insecurity, which are not great places to be when trying to lead a new family.

He was in a dark place where he felt like his identity had been stripped from him. He didn't know how to lead his wife, or what that even meant, apart from financial provision. And now that was gone.

However, Jacob did not stay in that dark place. With the help of some men in his life, he was able to dive into what his identity actually was in Christ and what spiritually leading his home meant. He identified his overall mission in life, which revolved around creating connection and inspiration, something that was lacking in his life as a child. He figured out a lot of what was now expected of him as a Godly husband. He was even able to use his talents and mission in creating connection and inspiration to help his wife out of a dark time in her career and life. He learned how to pursue her in ways that brought them much closer together, instead of just spending meaningless time with her as he had been.

Jacob leaned in to what God said of him, what God was calling him to in his marriage and overall life in general, and was able to climb out of the dark hole and eventually lead his wife into a fruitful marriage. Everyday isn't always perfect, but its better now that he has a solid grasp on his mission and purpose!

EXPERIENCE

- Read 1 Peter 1:13, Ezekiel 28:7, and 2 Timothy 2:16-17
- Now that you know your calling, as it relates to marriage and fatherhood, what is one measurable step, that you can take in the next week to prepare yourself for this task? Make sure it is something that you can measure: you should know whether you did it or you didn't. For example: "I am going to read 2 chapters of the Bible every day." This is measurable. Saying "I am going to be a better man this week" is not.
- Read Hebrews 13:20-21 and Psalm 86. Pray these prayers for yourself.

Be strong, and show yourself a man,
and keep the charge of the Lord your
God, walking in his ways and keeping
his statutes...

1 Kings 1:2-3

CHAPTER 3
Purging Sin & Obstacles

1 Kings 2:13-46

SIN

SIN PERVADES EVERYTHING ON THIS earth. It gets into our lives, takes root, and jeopardizes everything we seek to build. Leading a family is no exception.

The first and most obvious example of this is the sin that we, as men, struggle with ourselves. Lust and sexual immorality are the most glaring, but there are many ways we fall to sin. Greed, lust for power, dealing poorly with our anger, and being passive are just a few examples that are common. The second example is directly tied to the first as it is probably the reason you commit the sin in the first place: the false beliefs in yourself that drive you to fulfill needs in your life in sinful ways. The third is outright outside attacks on your family.

We need to purge our kingdom of this sin. I am not just talking about behavior modification, either. Usually, the sins we struggle with on a daily basis are rooted in something deep inside us that has been wounded, usually at a young age. I mentioned wounds at the beginning of the last chapter. One way we deal with wounds is creating a mission in life around them. The other way is that we unconsciously let them control us. We will go about "treating" that wound throughout our lives by any means available, and usually we will find certain things that treat it "better." This is fertile ground for sin to take place. And many times, our sin is addressing a very real, legitimate need. An addiction to pornography can be the result of a need to feel affirmation and connection. Greed and a lust for power can be the result of a need to feel validation as a man. Uncontrolled anger can be the result of being told that, as good Christians, we should never be angry. Eventually, this suppressed anger will begin to "come out sideways" in very unhealthy and possibly destructive ways. Passiveness can come from insecurity or fear of rejection, which itself is probably rooted in a wound where you have been rejected in the past. It is a very quiet sin that we commit when we are trying to protect ourselves. So, again, this one is rooted in a need for affirmation and a desire to feel safe.

We have to identify these roots. Once they are identified, we can begin to address the needs they present in healthy ways. They won't just go away. After all, the needs themselves are not inherently bad, just the sinful ways we have gone about fulfilling them.

So how do we do this? The truth is that you *probably* already know where these roots are. The majority of people, myself included, know where we were "wounded" as children. You probably know which parts of how you were raised shaped the behavior you now exhibit. This can be anything from a critical parent not allowing you to ever feel good enough to an abuser completely overpowering you and making you feel worthless, used, and disgusting. An absent father making you feel unwanted. A coach demanding perfection. The list goes on. But the point is we all have wounds. No one escapes childhood and adolescence without them.

If you don't know the root, then it may take some work to identify it. This can look many different ways. Counseling is a great start. Intensive weekends like The Unknown Weekend[1] or The Crucible Project[2] are great at helping you identify these roots as well. It may be as easy as journaling regularly about what triggers your sin and figuring out what need is being addressed by doing that sin.

There are always better, healthy ways in addressing these root needs in your life that aren't sinful. These ways usually aren't easy, but they are fulfilling. The best way to do it is to look to Scripture and what God has to say about you, and let that sink in and start to believe it. There is nothing more affirming than knowing that the Creator of the world loves you, so much so that He sent His only Son to die for you.

There are other ways as well. Find other men you trust and mentors you respect to speak truth into your life. We may have trouble seeing the good in us, but the ones closest to us can point it out. Let them speak into that and affirm you. It is very important to have a strong group of men around you that love you. Proverbs 27:17: "Iron sharpens iron, and one man sharpens another." The men we surround ourselves with are

---

[1] The Unknown Weekend is put on by an organization (Liminal) I trust that takes men on a very personal journey to identify the hidden parts of their lives. Visit theunknownweekend.org to find out more.
[2] The Crucible Project initial weekend is a similar experience to The Unknown Weekend. This weekend experience and the work in groups afterwards has completely changed my life. Visit thecrucibleproject.org to find out more.

very important in whether we are successful in rooting out the sin that has taken over our lives or not.

Another way that sin can attack our kingdom is from the outside. Satan is constantly looking to disrupt God's intentions. What better way than to attack marriage, a representation of Christ's love for the Church and God's intimacy with the Son and Holy Spirit? There will be many attempts in the life of your family by Satan to forcefully or manipulatively take what has been given to you by God.

This is a key part of being the spiritual leader of your home: being the *spiritual protector* of your home. When most men think of being their family's protector, they think of having a safe full of guns to fight off home invasions or potential boyfriends of their daughter. Or they think of a killer security system, a top safety rated car, and punching anyone in the face who ogles their wife. And while all of these things are good (except maybe the punching in the face...make sure you can justify that in a court of law) they do not capture the entire picture of protection. Spiritual warfare is real and you need to be ready when it comes to your kingdom.

This starts with knowing the hearts of the people in your house. And the only way to know them is to be invested in their nurturing. Sin can enter in from anywhere in your household. After all, it is filled with sinful people. You are ultimately responsible to God for allowing this sin to take hold.

It may seem unfair, but this is what you are signing up for. This is the responsibility that God has given you as a husband and father. Adam, the first man, found this out the hard way.

After Eve ate the forbidden fruit, and then Adam ate it, this happened:

> And they heard the sound of the Lord God walking in the garden in the cool of the day, and the man and his wife hid themselves from the presence of the LORD God among the trees of the garden. But the LORD God called to the man and said to him, "Where are you?" (Genesis 3:8-9)

God wanted to talk to Adam, not Eve, who technically sinned first. Who sinned doesn't seem to matter. Adam was ultimately responsible for the sin because he did not spiritually protect his wife from the temptations of Satan. And something else that is interesting is that he could have! In verse 6, it says, "she took of its fruit and ate, and she also gave some to her husband who was with her, and he ate." He was right there! That's the most essential step to protecting your family and he still messed it up. *You must be present in the lives of the members of your family to know how and when to protect them, and then when the need arises, you have to have the courage to actually protect them.*

Be active in the lives of your wife and kids. Know each of their struggles, insecurities, fears, and what is influencing them from outside and deal with them in grace. I'm not saying to be a strict, overbearing husband and father. That only really works with behavior modification and only while they fear you, which they eventually won't. Relate to them. Understand why they struggle with the sins that they do. A son will respond much better knowing that you, too, struggle with lust than he will if you just punish him severely when you find out that he has been looking at porn. That will most likely only lead to a secretive and destructive habit. Address the same root causes in him that you hopefully addressed in yourself. A wife will respond much better to a husband who strives to understand her struggles with shame, insecurity, or the overwhelming feat of motherhood than she will to a husband who heaps even more shame on top. Point them to Scripture and what God has to say about their struggles and identities.

My oldest son, Jonah, recently started school. Usually when he gets home, he will just be the normal, happy person that he usually is. However, there are some days when he comes home and is in the worst mood ever. He is angry. He is overly sensitive. He is mean to his mom and his younger brother. Whenever I get to witness this, my initial instinct is to correct him. Make him stop being mean, either by raising my voice or putting him in timeout. I want to force better behavior, and when I try, all that usually happens is he gets even more upset. He is now just up in his room alone where I don't have to hear it. Nothing really changes. What I have found is that when he is like this, there is probably something else going on underneath the surface. True, sometimes he's just tired and cranky from a long day at school. However, at other times, when I take the time to ask him what is really going on, and attempt to draw some information out of him, I find out something that makes it all come together.

Once, earlier in the day at recess, someone had said something to him that hurt his feelings and the teachers didn't really handle it well and it had been eating at him all day. Being six, he didn't really know how to express that very well, or even know that that was what was going on. As a dad who loves his son, it was my job to help him figure that out so that he could learn how to direct the energy in the right way in the future and not at his little brother. It was also a good opportunity to relate to him by letting him know that people say things to me that make me upset sometimes, too. But taking that out on the wrong people isn't the best way to deal with it.

Sometimes, though, they still won't respond in the way you want them to. But you have to keep trying. More than likely, your repeated attempts will eventually break through. Like I said before, a ship does not change direction immediately. You signed up for a lifetime of spiritual leadership, not just for the times when it is easy.

Grace is of utmost importance when dealing with the fallen nature of the people God has entrusted you to lead. But that does not mean that correction and discipline are not at all needed. But always do so in love, and not out of a place of resentment. Anger is not a sin in and of itself, but make sure that you are expressing that anger cleanly and lovingly.

SOLOMON PURGES HIS ADMINISTRATION

Immediately following David's charge to his son to be a man of God, he gives him some very detailed instructions on what he should do to address some very real threats to the kingdom's success. He gives him the name of two men that had wronged him in the past and were still hanging around ready to pounce on Solomon. Solomon takes this to heart and also identifies two other people that are also a threat. I want to look at each of these men and what they represented in Solomon's kingdom.

The application here is up to you. Since we are looking at Solomon's literal kingdom and the people in it as representative of you and your family, the exact parallel of these external attacks might not exist. The sin Adonijah represents in *Solomon's* kingdom might be *your* sin in your kingdom. The point I am driving home here is that there are sinful threats that show up in multiple ways. This is how they showed up in Solomon's kingdom and these same themes will show up in yours.

1. Adonijah – *Pride and Insecurity*

As mentioned before, Adonijah was Solomon's older half-brother (same dad, different mom) and heir-apparent to the throne after David because his older brothers had already died. However, since the actual successor is the choice of the king's, and David chose Solomon, Adonijah was left in the dust.

I can only imagine how this wounded Adonijah. It

probably went something like this: "Dad likes my brother a
lot more than me. I have lived most of my life in the shadow
of my older brothers, and now that I finally have my shot,
dad skipped over me to someone he liked more. I must not be
good enough."

This is a very common wound: not believing that you are
good enough. Most men have it in one way or another. The
ways we go about dealing with it are numerous, but Adonijah
utilizes some very common ones.

First, he developed a strong sense of entitlement. In an
effort to prove to himself that he was good enough, he (either
consciously or subconsciously) decided to just assume things
that made him feel better about himself, namely that he
was the rightful king. He thought that the kingdom was his
by rights, and everyone who thought otherwise was wrong.
This led to unhealthy pride in himself and very manipulative
techniques at securing what wasn't rightfully his.

Before David was dead and Solomon officially took the
throne, Adonijah gathered a group of people around him that
he believed would be able to help him secure the kingdom.
(These people included the commander of the army, Joab, and
the priest, Abiathar, whom we will learn about below.) They
began to form an army and met together to make sacrifices that
officially pronounced Adonijah king. Solomon and certain
others who were extremely loyal to King David were not
invited, confirming that Adonijah knew that he was rebelling
against David's wishes. His pride, in an effort to provide him
a feeling of accomplishment and importance and a knowledge

that he was good enough, would not let him humbly give the throne over to his younger brother.

When Solomon's mother, Bathsheba, and David's spiritual advisor, Nathan, brought this to the attention of David, he went ahead and declared Solomon king so that there would be no confusion, thus solidifying in Adonijah's mind that no, he was not good enough. This is where things get even messier.

Adonijah went into full manipulation mode. His pride, in another attempt to cover up his shortcomings and insecurities, came up with what he thought was a very sneaky way to steal the throne away from Solomon. By this point, David was dead and Solomon had been declared king. Adonijah cornered Bathsheba to solicit her unknowing help in dethroning her son.

He asked her if she would bring a request to King Solomon. If he were to bring the request directly, it would seem too obvious, so he preyed upon Bathsheba's naiveté. Adonijah then requested the hand of one of King David's concubines.[3]

This may not seem like that big of a deal given the circumstances. However, what this meant back then is very profound. For one reason or another, if someone were to marry one of the king's women, it strengthened his claim to the throne that the king was on. So this was a sneaky attempt for Adonijah to strengthen his claim to the throne. For some reason, Bathsheba didn't see this for what it was. I don't know why. Perhaps she had compassion for the concubine and

---

[3] For the time being, let's set aside any discussion of the morality of multiple wives, mistresses, and concubines. David had several. It is what it is. The morality of this fact is irrelevant in this application.

thought Adonijah would make a good husband now that her means of support were gone, much like hers was when her first husband died. Perhaps this is why Adonijah approached Bathsheba in the first place. Or maybe Adonijah knew he had a much better shot at Solomon listening to his mother than to his rival. I'm not sure, but the result was that Bathsheba took the bait and brought the request to Solomon.

Solomon didn't bite. He saw what was going on immediately. He was able to see past the trick and see Adonijah for what he was: a manipulative, prideful man that needed to be stopped.

As I said before, the exact application of this theme in your kingdom may be different. There may not be another person trying to manipulate you because they don't think they are good enough. You may be the person in your kingdom that is manipulative and prideful because of insecurity. Becoming aware of the belief that you are not good enough and how you typically go about dealing with that (i.e. manipulation to get what you want) is the most important step in changing that behavior in the future.

In the Bible, Solomon had Adonijah executed for his manipulation and pride. In the same way, you must do everything you can to identify and remove this threat. Philippians 2:3-4 says "Do nothing from selfish ambition or conceit, but in humility count others more significant than yourselves. Let each of you look not only to his own interests, but also to the interests of others."

2. Joab – *Uncontrolled Anger*

Joab was David's nephew and had been the commander of his army for a long time. He had a tendency to be hot-headed and not follow orders. David called out a couple of these examples while he is talking to Solomon:

> "Moreover, you also know what Joab the son of Zeruiah did to me, how he dealt with the two commanders of the armies of Israel, Abner the son of Ner, and Amasa the son of Jether, whom he killed, avenging in time of peace for blood that had been shed in war, and putting the blood of war on the belt around his waist and on the sandals on his feet. Act therefore according to your wisdom, but do not let his gray head go down to Sheol in peace." (1 Kings 2:5-6)

Abner had been the commander of an opposing army that was at war with David. During one battle, Abner killed Joab's brother. Later, Abner left the opposing army and swore allegiance to David. Joab was not too happy about this, and murdered Abner by stabbing him in the stomach in private to avenge his brother. David was not happy about this, but presumably out of loyalty to Joab, did not punish him at the time (2 Samuel 2-3).

Later, David replaced Joab with a guy named Amasa, another one of his nephews, as the commander of the army

(2 Samuel 19:13). This was strange because Amasa had been another opposing army commander against David during his son Absalom's rebellion (2 Samuel 17:25). David replaced Joab with Amasa most likely because Joab had disobeyed David and killed Absalom to end the war instead of capturing him alive (2 Samuel 18:1-18) and then publicly called David out when he was upset about it (2 Samuel 19:1-8). Joab obviously took issue with this. First of all, Amasa had committed treason by backing Absalom in the rebellion and was now apparently being rewarded for this behavior. Secondly, Joab was being demoted so that this traitor could take his place.

In an effort to restore his own dignity, Joab killed Amasa, stabbing him in the stomach (I'm sensing a trend here) and leaving him to bleed out on a road (2 Samuel 20). Joab was back in control. David, in his loyalty to Joab, again didn't punish him, but never forgot Joab's injustices. He knew that in order for Solomon to succeed in leading his kingdom, he would need to root out this out-of-control anger in his administration.

Again, much like with Adonijah, we can assume what was going through Joab's head and what led him to these decisions to murder these men. Joab worked loyally and extremely hard for David his entire life. He fought David's battles, kept David's secrets, killed David's enemies, and protected David's lands. However, he did not have an ounce of grace in his body. He did not understand why David pardoned his enemies over and over. I'm sure he was left with a feeling that no matter what he did, he just didn't matter. David was going to choose everyone else but him, even the enemy. David didn't seem to care that Abner had killed Joab's brother. David didn't seem to care that Amasa had committed treason. These men were not punished, but *rewarded*. Joab took it into his own hands to enact what he deemed was justice. He had to stand up for what *he* believed was right, even if it just caused more chaos. And all this he did in an effort to feel some sense of *identity*, to feel like he *mattered* and what he *did* mattered. How he did it, though, was through outright murder.

His first reaction to something wrong was always unjustifiable violence and anger. Don't get me wrong, there are plenty of times in life to be justifiably violent and angry. But with Joab, his timing was wrong. David even said it: "... [Joab] killed, avenging in time of peace for blood that had been shed in war." His anger and desire for vengeance was out of control.

Likewise, unchecked anger in your own life will cause massive destruction in your own family. This is another sin that must be rooted out and brought under control. Anger is not in and of itself evil, but it does have great potential to do a lot of harm, especially to the ones we love.

Or maybe you have a similar message running in your own head: "I don't matter." Maybe the ways you go about proving to yourself that you do matter are at the expense of the people around you. Do you run over others in an attempt to feel more important? Do you withhold grace and love for people because you don't think that they deserve it? If so, then this is probably a sign that you have a similar wound to Joab, and steps need to be taken to rectify it, or the people that it will fall out on will be your wife and kids.

3. Abiathar – *Fear and Passivity*

Abiathar had been a High Priest during the reign of David. He had been very loyal to David for many years, but for some reason chose to back Adonijah instead of Solomon as David was dying. Solomon stripped him of his priestly duties and banished him to live under house arrest for the rest of his life (1 Kings 2:26-27). I believe this treasonous choice for Abiathar was rooted in passivity, which itself was rooted in a wound from earlier in his life.

Over 40 years before, before David was king, he was on the run from the previous king, Saul. Saul wanted David dead because he knew that he was about to be replaced by him. Saul had found out that David had been helped by a community of priests led by the father of Abiathar, Ahimilech. There were 85 priests total. Saul had them all murdered, as well as everyone who lived in their community, including the women, children, and all the livestock. There was only one survivor, Abiathar, who somehow had escaped. He wisely teamed up with David following this, and David eventually made him High Priest (1 Samuel 22:6-23).

I can't even begin to imagine how this incredibly traumatic event impacted young Abiathar. Literally everyone he knew and loved were murdered before his eyes. He was probably feeling intense fear, sadness, and anger. He may have felt extreme guilt because he was the only survivor. He may have felt like he didn't do enough to save the others or that he actually did something *wrong*. My best guess is that he left that trauma feeling like someone who didn't believe that he deserved to live when others had died and that he had somehow messed up. He hadn't *loved* them in the right way, and everyone dying was the result. So, he did the only thing that made sense in the moment: run to someone who could protect *him*. David offered him safety in his time of need (1 Samuel 22:23). Don't get me wrong; this was exactly what he needed to do at this time! He was a victim and needed to find safety as soon as possible. It was the only thing he could have done. There is no blame to be placed on Abiathar in this specific circumstance.

However, forty or so years later, he appeared to still be letting this trauma effect his every decision. However you look at his decision to commit treason with Adonijah, I believe that it was rooted in passivity and self-protection which was itself rooted in the wound he had received forty some odd years before.

The first possibility is that he just went with the flow and supported Adonijah. Traditionally, the oldest living son was presumed to be king, as we have already discussed. Abiathar could have just assumed this was what was going to be decided, so he backed the traditional choice without ever being aware of what was really going on. If this was the case, he was being naïve and passive in his duties as the High Priest. As such, he should have known God and the king's true wishes (Solomon was to be king) and gone with them instead of someone without authority claiming something different. This was connected to the traumatic wound because he may have thought that if he did something wrong, other people could get hurt. So he fell back on tradition and legalism. Legalism is a type of passivity because you are putting the responsibility of your actions and decisions on a pre-determined list of rules instead of letting your choices be your choices. You are abdicating your choices and responsibility to what you *have* to do instead of what you *should* do (sometimes those can be the same; in this case, they were not).

A second possibility is that he was afraid to stand up for what he knew was right for very similar reasons. When he was younger, no matter what he did, everyone got killed. If he stood up for what was right, like his father had, everyone gets killed. It would be best, then, to just throw your hat in with whoever has the most power in any given circumstance. David was dying and seemed weak, and here came Adonijah with Joab, the army commander, supporting him. They even invited Abiathar in (1 Kings 1:19). Adonijah represented power and strength that wanted Abiathar involved. He probably felt safe with Adonijah. And since Abiathar had learned to run to whoever could protect him the best when he was young, this was the obvious choice now. The passivity manifested itself here in a way that let others make his decisions for him, again abdicating his choice and responsibility.

Solomon recognized this passivity in Abiathar and saw the destructive potential it had for his kingdom. Partially out of compassion for Abiathar and what he had gone through in his life, and partially because of the great things Abiathar had done in his life, Solomon did not have Abiathar killed. He did, however, remove him from his position of High Priest and put under house arrest for the rest of his life. (1 Kings 2:26)

Though Solomon himself was not passive in this, he knew that passivity of any kind must be rooted out, even when it comes from a deeply wounded place. No one could blame Abiathar for how his life turned out. He had, after all, been a victim in a horribly traumatic attack that left everyone he knew dead. There is not fault in Abiathar in the wound itself. The passivity came later because he had never fully taken responsibility for his own life. He chose to remain in that victim space and make his choices based on that. That is what needs to be rooted out of your kingdom.[4]

4. Shimei – *Shame*

Shimei is another person that David directly warned Solomon of and advised removing him:

> "And there is also with you Shimei the son
> of Gera, the Benjaminite from Bahurim,
> who cursed me with a grievous curse on the
> day when I went to Mahanaim. But when he
> came down to meet me at the Jordan, I swore
> to him by the LORD, saying, 'I will not put

---

[4] Disclaimer: trauma can lead to PTSD and other very serious psychological disorders. If this is the case for you or someone in your family, medical professionals should absolutely be brought in to help address these issues. I am not at all saying that if you have been through trauma, just get over it and take responsibility for your life and all your problems will go away. Trauma is very serious and should not be taken lightly. Visit nami.org (National Alliance for Mental Illness) to find help in your area. Taking responsibility does not mean saying that what happened shouldn't matter anymore. Taking responsibility does mean making choices for you to take steps forward in your life. That is the main application for this section I hope you leave with.

you to death with the sword. Now therefore
do not hold him guiltless, for you are a wise
man. You will know what you ought to do to
him, and you shall bring his gray head down
with blood to Sheol." (1 Kings 2:8-9)

The original story that David is referring to can be found
in 2 Samuel 16:5-14, with the final conclusion where David
pardoned Shimei being found in 2 Samuel 19:16-23. I'll give
you a quick summary.

David's son, Absalom, had just recently announced his
rebellion. David fled the city of Jerusalem with his people
because Absalom was gaining some steam and David was
attempting to avoid outright bloodshed in the city streets.
As David fled, he no doubt reflected on what got him to
this point. Absalom was rebelling because David had been a
terrible father. The whole Bathsheba incident had happened
before this as well, and David no doubt thought that this was
perhaps his punishment for all the evil he had done in his life
and as king. 2 Samuel 15:30 says that he was weeping as he
fled. The Hebrew word for "weeping" here can be translated
as "a penitent's weeping before the Lord." In other words,
he wasn't weeping because he was simply sad that Absalom
was rebelling; he was actually weeping because of what he had
done that had caused all this. He was feeling intense shame
and guilt for his sins.

And right then, at his low point, while he is fleeing the
result of his sin, is when Shimei shows up. Shimei had been

related to Saul, the king before David. He saw this opportunity of David at a low spot to take revenge on David for what he had done to his kinsmen, Saul. As David and his men marched, Shimei followed closely, hurling rocks, insults, and curses at David. "You are bloodthirsty. You are worthless. You are evil. God is doing this to you because you are so bad. (2 Samuel 16:7-8 paraphrase)." One of David's men, Abishai, offered to go take care of Shimei, but David said no. He actually let him stick around, hurling his judgments and insults. Verses 10 and 11 actually make it sound like David may have believed Shimei's assertion that God was punishing him for everything. Whatever the reason, David allowed this intense criticism and judgment to stick around and it says that when they finally arrived at where they were going, David was weary. Literally exhausted, as if he had been carrying a heavy load.

We don't hear about Shimei again until after the war. After David took back the kingdom from his son, Absalom, Shimei realized that the man he had cursed and insulted so ruthlessly was now back in charge. He came to David to beg for his life. Again, Abishai offered to kill Shimei. David declined the offer again, but for a different reason. Take a look at the different responses:

During David's flight from Jerusalem:

> "If he is cursing because the LORD has said to him, 'Curse David,' who then shall say, 'Why have you done so?'...Behold, my own son seeks my life; how much more now may

this Benjaminite! Leave him alone, and let him curse, for the LORD has told him to." (2 Samuel 16:10-11)

After the war:

"Shall anyone be put to death in Israel this day? For do I not know that I am this day king over Israel?" (2 Samuel 19:22)

He no longer believed what Shimei was saying about him. He believed something else: that he was king. He believed it because God said it about him, and the things Shimei said about him no longer held any weight. He was *king* and from that place he could govern the way that he wanted to: with grace.

However, David eventually saw the benefit in getting rid of Shimei for good or else he wouldn't have told Solomon to bring his "gray head down with blood to Sheol." I think that, though the lesson of having grace for our enemies is obviously present, there is another lesson here about what we should do with the false, shaming, accusatory messages that we hang onto in our lives. If we are going to view Shimei as representative of those messages, we can see that David allowed these messages to hang around his entire life, even when he knew they were no longer true. David was essentially telling Solomon to not let the wounds people afflict on him rule his life. Deal with those messages and put them to rest. Don't let those people rule your life anymore.

Curiously, Solomon let Shimei hang around for three more years under house arrest. But Shimei, like the shaming messages always do if we let them, poked his head up again by violating the conditions. Solomon finally had him put to death, effectively ending the "shame."

Now, I am obviously not telling you to kill the people who have shamed you in the past. What I am trying to say is that you have to get the shameful messages that run your life and keep you from your true power out of your head. You can't let them run your life anymore. David and Solomon eventually figured this out.

Perhaps the reason it is so hard to get these shaming messages out of our heads is because they actually have a lot of truth to them. David was a violent man who had killed people to get what he wanted (Goliath at one end of the spectrum and Uriah on the other). Sin does have consequences and this rebellion of Absalom's was *absolutely* a consequence of David's sin (passivity in fatherhood). However, we are not defined by what we have done, but by who God says we are. And we all regularly confuse the consequences of sin with punishment from God. Asking for forgiveness and receiving it while simultaneously taking responsibility for the sin and dealing with the consequences are not mutually exclusive. Grace does not make the actual action of the sin go away. Whatever you did is done, and it may be a lead domino that will affect your life down the road. It does, however, take the *punishment* away because God no longer holds it against us. It also confirms who we are in God's eyes. In David's case, he was still king and God still wanted him to be king. However, sometimes we can't forgive ourselves for what we have done, so another consequence of sin is shame.

The best way to kill off shame in your kingdom is by bringing whatever it is you are ashamed of out into the light. Shame is like a vampire that sucks the life out of you in darkness and in secret. It can't, however, survive in the light. Confession is the spiritual discipline that addresses this. James 5:16 says this: "... confess your sins to one another and pray for one another, so that you may be healed ..." Confessing our sins to God is great and necessary in order to get big G Grace. However, confessing our sins to other people is the way to get healing, or freedom from shame. Nothing kills shame faster than telling someone what you have done, expecting to be shamed more for it, but instead getting love and acceptance. So, as I have said before, and will say again, finding men in your life that will challenge you, but also give you grace and unconditional love and acceptance is extremely important in setting up your kingdom. They are the ones that can help you finally defeat the shame!

OVERCOMING FEAR AND SHAME

Pride, insecurity, uncontrolled anger, fear, passivity, and shame are some big obstacles that *will* pop up in your life that will keep you from being the spiritual leader your family needs.

The following is how a couple of these have shown up in a real life story from more recently than three thousand years ago.

This is my story.

I mentioned earlier that a while back my wife sat me down and told me that I was not being a good spiritual leader of our home. And she was right. I had become a very passive husband and father when it came to spiritual leadership. I had succumbed to the lie that being a husband and father simply meant providing money to buy food, clothing, and shelter, and protecting them from physical threats. I occasionally prayed with my wife, but only after following her suggestion that we should do so. I rarely encouraged my wife to get rest and fill her soul; I just let her friends take care of her in that regard. I left the Biblical education of my sons to their teachers in our church's kids ministry. I lashed out in anger a lot, trying to modify their bad behavior with power and fear. After all, the family wasn't falling apart; everything seemed to be going pretty fine. I was content with putting the whole thing on auto pilot and just hoping nothing terrible happened. Sure, as parents, we were stressed out and tired and our kids' behavior was on a slow decline, but nothing was falling apart.

Luckily, God used my wife to help open my eyes to the need for me to step up. It was during a conversation regarding something to do with a messy house, bad behavior at bed time, and a slew of other things that were eating away at our energy and patience. It seems small, but my wife needed a man at that point who would step up and lead our family out of the struggle before things got worse. And it absolutely terrified me.

I had known this about myself for some time, but I was hoping no one else would catch on and actually expect anything from me. The reason for this was fear. I was afraid to step up and be a man. And that fear was a result of Satan accusing me of what I used to be.

When I was in high school, I was diagnosed with depression and went on anti-depressants. They were supposed to help the sadness go away. They worked. I was no longer sad and hopeless all the time. However, they also numbed every other emotion as well. I didn't feel much of anything. I had been a very sensitive child, prone to every emotion and expression of those emotions. I cried a lot. I laughed a lot. But as time went on with that medication, I began to lose those emotions and expressions. Essentially, I stopped emotionally maturing around the age of 15.

I wasn't a zombie or anything like that. I could function. Just most of the emotions that I expressed were contrived. Occasionally I felt legitimate emotion, like at my wedding or the births of my two sons, but those moments were few and far between. And I lost a lot of passion for the things I once loved, like creating music and serving at church. When that happened, my faith went on cruise control. I found I had more of a desire to fit in with people I perceived as who I wanted to be, and this cut down on my evangelistic drive. I didn't want to talk to anybody about God because I didn't want them to think negatively of me and reject me. Once emotion and passion were out of the picture, life became a ladder of trying to achieve more and be popular. God took a backseat in my life.

Fast-forward to age 27. I had been on anti-depressants around twelve years at that point, slowly declining into a person without emotion who was unable to connect with people. A pharmacy mix-up caused me to go without my medication for three weeks. This may not seem like a big deal, but when you go cold turkey off any medication after twelve years, things can get weird. I began going through some pretty severe withdrawal symptoms: cold sweats, fevers that lasted 30 minutes and would then vanish, brain zaps (crazy electrical impulses that shoot through your brain occasionally and leave you feeling disoriented). And then the grand-daddy symptom of them all, the one I least expected and was least prepared for: actual emotion.

I became irritable with *everyone*, all the time. I had mood swings and temper tantrums. I was unbelievably sad. I was unbelievably angry. And I had no idea what to do with it. About two and a half weeks after I went off the meds, while standing during worship during church one weekend, I began to cry uncontrollably. I had no idea what was going on with me. It scared me. It also scared my wife, who was standing beside me.

We left immediately and went to talk somewhere. In that conversation, I had to admit some things. Mood swings and irritability aside, I had no idea what to do with this emotion that was bubbling to the surface. I never learned how to handle it because I numbed it all when I was 15. I had started to rely on the medication to protect me from everything instead of relying on God. It had become a crutch.

That next week I went to my doctor and we figured it out. I went on half the dosage that I was taking before. Depression was still a real thing in my life and I wanted it under control, but I didn't want the medication to control all of me. The lower dosage has been great, and I can still feel the full range of emotions, but the overwhelming sadness and hopelessness that comes with depression is easier to handle because of the pills. But I learned that day that a sole reliance on chemicals to fix me was not enough. I needed to let God back in as well.

Now, fast-forward again to age 29, when she had this conversation with me. I was feeling all of the emotions and have very healthy practices in place to know how to express and deal with them. I was becoming a better communicator with my wife, something that was very much lacking when I was emotionless. But in one area I was still withholding vulnerability and communication with her and my kids: spiritual leadership.

I was terrified to step into that. Messages and lies that I wasn't what they needed controlled that area of my life. I knew they needed it, but was afraid that if I tried, they would laugh at me and tell me, "Nice try, but we know you're just an emotionless boy who can't actually tell us anything useful at all. And it's probably just contrived concern and love for us, anyway. You're just trying to look the part of 'spiritual leader,' but you can't actually be a real one. You are not enough."

This is what kept me from stepping into spiritual leadership. Fear of rejection and a reminder of who I used to be. Satan was using that to effectively attack my kingdom, and if I hadn't gotten ahold of it, I could have lost everything.

That is what prompted me to figure out exactly what spiritually leading my home meant and eventually led to me writing this book. It seems crazy to me that I am writing this. Someone as emotionless and fearful as I used to be is clearly not a qualified candidate to speak to anyone else about how to do it right. But those are just Satan's accusations popping up again. I *am* the man that my family needs. God entrusted me with them, and however unqualified I may be on my own, He has put me here for a reason and will equip me and qualify me.

You are the man that your family will need (or needs right now). Do not let Satan's accusations and reminders keep you from being the man that God has called you to be. God is with you, and hopefully some other men are with you as well to encourage you and spur you on.

That is an essential piece to this that I want to reiterate one more time: the importance of having Godly men around you. After Solomon removed the sinful and manipulative people from his administration, he didn't just leave it empty. He filled it with men that he trusted: prophets who acted as mentors to guide him and peers that loved him and spoke truth to him (see 1 Kings 4:1-19 for the list).

The same is necessary for you. As men, we are made to run to other men when we need help. If those men aren't Godly, or if those men won't speak truth to you, it is better to go it alone. But that is not the most ideal way to do things. Find a mentor who will help guide you. Choose a few friends that you trust who can call you on your crap, support you in your struggles, and love you for who you *are*, not who you *were*. Meet with them regularly and be completely open with them. Like I said before, shame loses its power when it is shared with someone who accepts and loves you no matter what. Share your emotions and frustrations, as well as your triumphs and successes. Let these Godly men sharpen you, and take to heart their counsel.

Finding this group of men can be tricky. The obvious way you would expect someone like me to tell you to find them is through your church's small groups program, if there is one. And yes, that is a good option. However, I understand that it is also a risky option. You never know who is going to show up to those things, if you will get along with them at all, or if you can trust them. If you are going to go that route, which again, I believe is a good option, I would advise getting to know the people in that group before fully trusting them with all your baggage. There are few things worse than finding out too late that you can't trust someone with delicate information.

Another route, which is the one I've taken, is by going deeper with the men that are already around you. You may not be the best of friends yet, but that's okay. Trust and relationship building takes time and energy. Over time, the natural tendency to go deeper will arrive and you will find yourself with some men in your life who are serious about being there for you, as you are for them.

JESUS OVERCAME OBSTACLES

Jesus never sinned, which doesn't mean that He didn't know how to overcome obstacles. Instead, it means He was *perfect* at overcoming obstacles.

The Bible is very clear on the fact that Jesus did have temptation in His life. Hebrews tells us, "For we do not have a high priest who is unable to sympathize with our weaknesses, but one who in every respect has been tempted as we are, yet without sin" (Hebrews 4:15). So, how exactly did Jesus combat the sin that tried to sabotage His ministry?

The Gospels lay out an account of Jesus' temptation in the wilderness, found in Matthew 4 and Luke 4. Those stories tell us that Satan tempted Jesus three times. One way was tempting Him through his flesh and bodily needs. Jesus was fasting from food, so He was hungry, and Satan tempted Him to turn rocks to bread. Another way was through power. He told Jesus that he could give Him authority over all of the kingdoms of the world if He would just bow down and worship Satan. The last way was an attempt to make Jesus question God's protection and put Him to the test.

The way Jesus combatted each of these temptations was with Scripture. He had studied it His whole life and knew what it said. He knew the truth that it proclaimed about God, and the better way of life that it lays out. Having that firm foundation of wisdom and truth through Scripture, He was able to nip temptation in the bud, before it ever grew into sin.

He also combatted the sin that tried to steal His people away. In the Gospels, Jesus constantly confronts the Pharisees and warns His people to stay away from them. The Pharisees were a poison to the Kingdom of God. They were highly hypocritical leaders who loaded everyone with heavy burdens of rules they couldn't fully follow. Then, they loaded them up with shame when they inevitably failed. Jesus loved His followers, his future Church, and He knew the terrible lies and hypocrisy the Pharisees were selling. The people were becoming convinced that God only cared about the *way* people did things, not *why*. Rules were to be followed so that you *looked* like a good follower of God. But the heart of true worship was never addressed by the Pharisees.

Jesus wanted His people to truly be in step with God, but they were being led astray by people who were trying to convince them that they only needed to look the part. He rebuked the Pharisees for being nitpicky about the laws that said that people had to wash their hands before eating a meal, or else they would be unclean in Mark 7, again using Scripture:

> And he said to them, "Well did Isaiah
> prophesy of you hypocrites, as it is written,
> 'This people honors me with their lips,
>   but their heart is far from me;
> in vain do they worship me,
>   teaching as doctrines the
> commandments of men.'
> You leave the commandment of God and
> hold to the tradition of men." (Mark 7:6-8)

A few verses later, he addresses His people:

> And he called the people to him again and said
> to them, "Hear me, all of you, and understand:
> There is nothing outside a person that by
> going into him can defile him, but the things
> that come out of a person are what defile
> him." (Mark 7:14-15)

He wanted to be very clear with His followers. God cares about the heart, not all the frivolous traditions. The people were deceived into a lie from the outside, and Jesus was not going to stand for it in His kingdom.

Jesus also had to confront His emotional distress. In the Garden of Gethsemane, as He was praying to God, looking ahead to what was to come the next day, He prayed that God would "remove this cup" from Him. It says that He was "in agony" while praying, and that He even began to sweat blood, a sign of severe stress.

But even in His distress, He still deferred to the Father. "Not my will, but yours, be done," He prays. He still knew that God had a purpose and a plan because He knew God. And most importantly, He still obeyed and went through with it. After all, that was His mission and calling, and He was fully committed to fulfilling it.

Jesus also had a strong group of men around Him. He was obviously the strongest, but He still modeled this for us. These twelve men, save Judas, went on to establish the Church in the

Book of Acts with the help of the Holy Spirit, so they weren't just a bunch of lowlifes without a clue about anything. Jesus built into them, and they were there to support Him when He needed it, though they often failed at this. The point is that Jesus surrounded Himself with men that He loved and trusted, and that is vital for us as well when we are setting up a kingdom of our own.

ADAM'S STORY

Adam is newly married, but only by the grace of God, his wife, and a few close men. He is 28 now but most of his young adult life was spent in the partying scene. Sex, drugs, alcohol. You name it, Adam tried it and liked it.

Once he came to know Jesus, he knew some things had to change. The partying had been feeding him acceptance and value for a long time. The altered state of mind caused him to do some things he was ashamed of, which led to a need for more acceptance (to numb the shame) and therefore more partying. It was a constant cycle of acceptance and shame. What he was really looking for, however, was that deep well of satisfaction and joy that only true connection with God and faithful friends and family can provide.

Thankfully, he had been on this better path for a couple of years. He had those men in his life that could speak affirmation to him. He had connection with friends and family. He had also gotten engaged to a wonderful woman. Everything was going great.

But as I talked about before, the enemy likes to remind us often of who we used to be. And at the wrong moment, the results can be disastrous.

One night, Adam was at a party and had a few drinks. Feeling particularly down that day, he decided to keep drinking. And drinking. Until he was good and properly drunk. So drunk, in fact, that many parts of that night are hazy. Now, by the grace of God, nothing absolutely heinous happened except perhaps making a fool of himself in front of people who respected him. But the fact remained that he had gotten drunk and was only able to piece together what all happened from what other people told him the next day. This was not the type of behavior Adam wanted in his life anymore.

What's more is that his fiancée had never seen this side of him. She was aware of his colorful past, but to get a taste of it still happening rightfully scared her and gave reason to question whether she wanted to enter into a marriage with him. Her trust in him began to crumble.

Adam wasn't a bad person because of this. He had made a mistake and fallen back into a bad habit to mistakenly get the acceptance he was looking for. He eventually built that trust back by approaching the group of men in his life and asking for some support. Since these men were there for him no matter what, as he had been for some of them in the past, there was no shame involved. Just unconditional love and a drive to push Adam beyond what he was capable of on his own.

Adam leaned on these men and together they came

up with a plan to build trust back with his fiancée. This included a completely apologetic approach to a conversation with her (instead of a defensive one), a drinking fast to check his motives, and regular emotional check-ins with his circle of men and his fiancée so that he could be aware of what was going on inside of him. This way he would be able to find acceptance and value proactively instead of letting his past behaviors take over in a time of need. Her trust was repaired when she saw the steps he was willing to take to get back in integrity and the support he had from trustworthy men in his life.

EXPERIENCE

- What do you foresee getting in the way of you fulfilling the calling that God has given to you and having a thriving kingdom?
- Give that obstacle a voice. What does it say about who you are as a man that makes you inadequate to fulfill this calling?
- Where in your life have you seen these obstacles before?
- Read Philippians 4:13, 19, and 1 John 2:13.
- What does God have to say about you and your ability to fulfill your calling?

*For we do not have a high priest who
is unable to sympathize with our
weaknesses, but one who in every
aspect has been tempted as we are, yet
without sin.*

Hebrews 4:15

CHAPTER 4
Blessing

1 Kings 3:1-15
Matthew 7:7-11

A BLESSING OUT OF
WEAKNESS

THE SCARIEST MOMENT OF MY LIFE came in June of 2018. Eden, my daughter, had been born about a week before and I decided to take my two sons, Jonah (five years old at the time) and Carter (three) up to the family cabin for the day to give my wife a break from the toddler chaos and give Jonah and Carter some much needed dad time. My dad and some friends were already up there and we planned on having some fun.

It was a beautiful day so the boys and I went on a hike. There is a small waterfall about a half mile from the cabin that they love to go to and throw rocks in the creek. We set off nonchalantly like we had done a thousand times before, excited to get to the waterfall and goof around. About a third of the way there, literally still in view of the cabin, all the fun and excitement ended. A massive bull moose walked around from behind a big bush and stood right in the middle of the path, facing us, about ten to fifteen yards away.

If you've never seen one of these guys up close, allow me to paint you a picture. Ten yards away from me and my three and five year old sons stood a seven-foot tall, 1200 pound beast of nature. His legs alone towered above my sons' heads and his shoulders were a foot above mine. This moose was massive. And he was not happy.

Our cheerful meandering down the path had spooked him out of his quiet hiding place and the only clear path to safety was down the same path we had just come. Unfortunately I had the same idea.

For a few seconds all any of us did was freeze. Me, the moose, my boys. Frozen in fear and trying to figure out what to do next. Then, the moose moved. At first slowly, and then picking up pace, right towards us. I quickly turned my sons around and told them to go, go, go, GO! GO! RUUUNNN!

I could hear the massive hooves behind us, getting closer. Carter, the three year old, was not going fast enough so I leaned over and scooped him up. Jonah was booking it, but none of us were fast enough. We made it to a little shed next to the path and I dipped in next to it with Carter, but Jonah didn't see us and I couldn't reach him.

He kept running down the path.

So did the moose.

I watched in horror as the moose gained on my five-year old little boy. Feeling helpless, all I could do was scream "NOOOOO!!!" as the moose barreled down on Jonah, obscuring my view of him. Jonah fell down. I couldn't breathe.

The moose ran on and Jonah was laying off to the side

of the path. I carried Carter as I ran as fast as I could over to Jonah, not knowing what I was going to find.

Thank God he was okay. At least physically. The moose had run by him a couple of feet away. The sheer force of him running by had knocked Jonah down, but luckily the moose had no intentions that day of trampling anybody. But Jonah was traumatized, laying on the ground, crying his eyes out. Carter didn't seem as phased by the incident, as he turned to me and asked, "Dad, are mooses real?!?" Yes, Carter, they are very, VERY real.

Jonah, on the other hand, had a better handle on what had just happened. I carried him back to the porch of the cabin, wiped away the dirt, and began trying to pick up the pieces of a terrified little boy. He was angry and scared. But most gut-wrenching to me was that he thought that he had done something wrong. He believed that he hadn't been brave enough.

I sat there and held him and tried to explain, "Buddy, you did *nothing* wrong. You were so brave and did the only thing you knew to do, which was run. I know you are scared. Jonah, I was terrified as well. I have never been more scared in my entire life. It is okay to be scared by something like that."

He let me know that he wanted to go home and never come back to the cabin. I completely understood. Part of me never wanted to come back as well. But at that moment was a very unique opportunity for me. I had a chance to teach him about facing your fears and overcoming the perceived weakness we feel in life, and overcoming seemingly insurmountable obstacles.

I also didn't want to push him too hard because I knew that something traumatizing had just occurred. But that was just as much for me as it was for him.

You see, I had never felt as weak and helpless as I just had when that moose was running down my son. There was absolutely nothing I could do in the moment to change what was happening. I was doubting myself as a father and protector. There was something that I should have done differently, and because I didn't, my son almost died. I was terrified, weak, and a failure. I was ignorant because I didn't know what I *should* have done when charged by a moose. Obviously, booking it in the opposite direction probably wasn't the best choice. But it is all I could think of in the few seconds I had to decide. But the fact that I hadn't adequately prepared for such a circumstance was eating at me.

But I knew that if I didn't face *my* fears, he would never know how to face his. I had to lead by example right then, however hard that may be.

I told him, "Jonah, the only way we can face our fears right now is to show ourselves that we can make it to that waterfall. I know you are terrified, but we can't let that moose keep us from having the fun we came up here to have."

"Dad, I'm not brave enough. I'm not as brave as you."

"You know what, Jonah? I'm scared too. That moose absolutely terrified me," I answered.

He looked at me after I said that with confusion on his face. "You are scared too?"

I assured him, "Yes, absolutely terrified. But the only way to overcome that fear is to set out and do what we came here to do." Then I quoted Ned Stark of Game of Thrones, because who else would you quote at this point (I told you I was a fantasy nerd)? "Jonah, *the only time we can be brave is when we are scared.*"

That seemed to resonate with him as he realized that his dad was afraid too, but that didn't mean not brave. And that he could also be brave, even though he was afraid.

In my mind, I was spinning. Am I really going to walk back up that path knowing what just happened? Am I crazy? Am I pushing him too far? Is this worth it? Can't we just go back to the city and live out our lives in comfort with no fear of moose?

I prayed this in my mind: "God, give me the strength to face this fear and show my sons that they, too, can face their fears." I then grabbed a gun and did some quick research on what to do when confronted by a moose (head for the trees so they can't chase you as easily) and we again prepared for our hike to the waterfall. We also knew where the moose had gone to, so I wasn't very afraid that the same situation would happen again. But I wasn't leaving unprepared and naïve again.

We set out, a bit timidly, but also with confidence. We were going to have fun at the waterfall if was the last thing we did. As we hiked (my head on a swivel) we talked about moose, safety, what to do if we ran into another moose, bravery, fear, God's strength, and how proud of him I was. By the time we got to the waterfall, he was back to his old self. The creek got served a lot of rocks that day. Carter was there too, still contemplating his new found knowledge of the reality of "mooses."

There are some things in life we just can't do on our own. Being brave in the face of extreme fear and weakness is one of those things. Being a successful spiritual leader of our home is another.

Fortunately, God does not leave us to fend for ourselves in this. He offers us divine blessings and gifts to supplement our shortcomings. There is no way I could have walked back up that path with my own strength. The risk was too high. But with God's strength, I was able to not only face my fears, but help my five-year-old son face his and come out of the entire situation stronger.

Solomon learned this shortly after he had finished purging his administration. God appeared to Solomon one night in a dream and offered him a blessing of his choosing. Solomon took this opportunity to fortify himself where he was weak and insecure:

> And now, O LORD my God, you have made
> your servant king in place of David my father,
> although I am but a little child. I do not
> know how to go out or come in. And your
> servant is in the midst of your people whom

you have chosen, a great people, too many
to be numbered or counted for multitude.
Give your servant therefore an understanding
mind to govern your people, that I may
discern between good and evil, for who is able
to govern this your great people?" (1 Kings
3:7-9)

It is important to be aware of your shortcomings. It is also
important to ask God to supplement those shortcomings. I
had to acknowledge that I was weak in the face of a gargantuan
moose, and ask God to give me strength to be who my son
needed me to be at that moment. Solomon was aware that he
was young and was not knowledgeable enough to fulfill the
task of governing an entire kingdom on his own, so he asked
God to give him wisdom and knowledge so that he could be a
good king. God was very pleased with this choice of blessing:

It pleased the Lord that Solomon had asked
this. And God said to him, "Because you have
asked this, and have not asked for yourself
long life or riches or the life of your enemies,
but have asked for yourself understanding
to discern what is right, behold, I now do
according to your word. Behold, I give you a
wise and discerning mind, so that none like
you has been before you and none like you
shall arise after you. I give you also what you

have not asked, both riches and honor, so that
no other king shall compare with you, all your
days. And if you will walk in my ways, keeping
my statutes and my commandments, as your
father David walked, then I will lengthen your
days." (1 Kings 3:10-14)

Not only did God give Solomon the blessing he asked for,
he also gave him a ton of blessings that he didn't ask for. The
truth that is important to point out here is that God wants
to help us, and He wants to help us more than we could ever
imagine.

And what's more is that He offers us the same opportunity
for a blessing. In Matthew 7, Jesus says this:

"Ask, and it will be given to you; seek, and you
will find; knock, and it will be opened to you.
For everyone who asks receives, and the one
who seeks finds, and to the one who knocks
it will be opened. Or which one of you, if
his son asks him for bread, will give him a
stone? Or if he asks for a fish, will give him
a serpent? If you then, who are evil, know
how to give good gifts to your children, how
much more will your Father who is in heaven
give good things to those who ask him!"
(Matthew 7:7-11)

This wasn't a one-time deal just for Solomon. God also wants us to ask Him for what we need to accomplish our calling. And God won't stop at just providing that.

In the chapter before, Jesus is teaching about how to deal with anxiety. People were apparently worried about how they would feed and clothe themselves and their families. Jesus says to stop worrying and "seek first the kingdom of God and his righteousness, and all these things will be added to you" (Matthew 6:33).

If we trust God and ask for blessings that will help us in our calling and mission of being the spiritual leader of our home, and not for blessings meant simply to glorify ourselves, He will provide in ways beyond our comprehension. Humbly come before God and ask for a blessing that will strengthen you where you are weak. Are you afraid? Ask for courage and confidence. Do you see yourself as somebody without any knowledge or wisdom? Ask for wisdom. Are you tired? Ask for strength and perseverance. Are you stressed out and full of anxiety? Ask for peace.[1]

James tackles wisdom head on, in this regard: "If any of you lacks wisdom, let him ask God, who gives generously to all without reproach, and it will be given him" (James 1:5). Wherever it is that you are weak, God has a blessing that can support you, and He wants to give it. The only stipulation is that you humble yourself to ask for it. As the book of 1 Peter says:

---

[1] Disclaimer: Anxiety is often a symptom of something deeper psychologically going on, which is above my paygrade and the scope of this book. The anxiety I am referring to here is the more general "worry" that we do have control of. If the psychological variety of anxiety is what is troubling you, I would absolutely advise seeking medical guidance in navigating that.

> Likewise, you who are younger, be subject to the elders. Clothe yourselves, all of you, with humility toward one another, for "God opposes the proud but gives grace to the humble." Humble yourselves, therefore, under the mighty hand of God so that at the proper time he may exalt you, casting all your anxieties on him, because he cares for you. (1 Peter 5:5-7)

Pride can be a tough thing to overcome as men. The world expects us to have everything figured out and be strong enough on our own to meet any challenge that presents itself. Overcoming this pride is a major part to receiving blessing.

Admit to yourself that you don't have everything figured out. If you blindly press on thinking that you can go it alone and be successful, then whatever you are setting out to do may fall apart. Owning your weaknesses and shortcomings does not mean that you are not a man. Owning them presents the only real situation where you can actually be a man. The apostle Paul says it this way in 2 Corinthians:

> But [Jesus] said to me, "My grace is sufficient for you, for my power is made perfect in weakness." Therefore I will boast all the more gladly of my weaknesses, so that the power of Christ may rest upon me. For the sake of Christ, then, I am content with

weaknesses, insults, hardships, persecutions, and calamities. For when I am weak, then I am strong. (1 Corinthians 2:9-10)

Owning our weaknesses, and allowing God to supplement those weaknesses, and then proving successful despite those weaknesses shows the world that God is great, not us. The temptation here is to hope that we will be glorified by our accomplishments, but since we are not the ones who made those accomplishments possible, God gets all of the credit. And that is very important to know when entering into a family.

The purpose of our existence and the existence of our families is to glorify God. One of the ways we do this is by letting God use us to accomplish great things; things so great that no one can look at them and say, "Man, that guy is awesome!"

He wants to help us accomplish great things so that people will say, "There is no way that guy did that on his own!" People will see these accomplishments and either praise God, because they already know Him, or seek to find out who helped you, leading them straight to Jesus.

Solomon wasn't given wisdom, knowledge, riches, and power by God to glorify *Solomon*. He was given those gifts to glorify *God*! His kingdom grew to be one of the wealthiest and successful kingdoms of the ancient world, and everyone in the world knew who that kingdom worshiped: God.

JESUS COULD DO NOTHING WITHOUT THE FATHER

Jesus understood that without the blessing and direction of the Father, He could do nothing. Jesus says in the Gospel of John,

> "Truly, truly, I say to you, the Son can do nothing of his own accord, but only what he sees the Father doing. For whatever the Father does, that the Son does likewise. For the Father loves the Son and shows him all that he himself is doing. And greater works than these will he show him, so that you may marvel ... "I can do nothing on my own. As I hear, I judge, and my judgment is just, because I seek not my own will but the will of him who sent me." (John 5:19-20, 30)

Philippians 2 tells us that Jesus did not consider equality with God something to be grasped, even though he was God. This is a great model for us as humans. We are not God and cannot do anything on our own. We are subject to the will and commands of God, just as Jesus was and we can do nothing without His blessings and strengths.

Not even Jesus, who had more reason than anybody, had pride enough to assume He could go it alone. He did as the Father commanded and continuously asked for His help. Do not fool yourself into thinking that God will reward you for trying to do it by yourself. Swallow your pride and ask for

God's blessing to help you where you are weak. Perhaps even more foreign, ask for the help of other Godly men around you.

JOHN'S STORY

My friend, John, was young, single, and in serious debt. He worked at a very posh and competitive financial planning firm. Being new to the profession, he had a desire to fit in with everyone else there. This meant buying really nice things to keep up with those around him. Nice suits, a car, excessive spending on work trips. He threw it all on credit cards, and when one would max out, he would just open another.

He had been denying that there was a problem at all for a long time. But soon he found himself at the bottom of a deep hole with no way out on his own. Wanting to start a family eventually, he realized that doing so from down in the bottom of a pit was not the best way to go about it. He needed someone to come down in the hole with him, sift through all the dirt, and help him find a way out.

Fortunately for John, our church had a financial counselor on staff who was willing to do just that. With a prayer for courage and an email to the counselor, he started the long, hard climb out of the hole. He and the counselor met one afternoon for a couple of hours as John laid out everything. Credit card statements, pay stubs, every monthly expense John had, every receipt for each frivolous purchase. It was not a pretty sight.

But hitting the bottom rarely is. John had the wisdom to realize that something in his life wasn't working and to continue on doing the same thing would not set himself up for success in marriage down the road. He had to own that his choices had landed him in this current situation, and his future choices would need to look different.

John did just that. He identified this weakness in his life, asked for help, and is making serious strides toward fixing the issue based on the advice of the financial counselor. His career is beginning to take off, and though a family isn't in the cards just yet, his newfound financial maturity is a blessing that one day they will be extremely grateful for.

EXPERIENCE

- What are your weaknesses? Where are you insecure in your spiritual leadership?
- In an effort to swallow your pride, find a man you trust and tell him about that weakness and the fears/insecurities it produces in regard to leading your family.
- Pray to God and ask Him to fortify you in that area.

CHAPTER 5
Living Out Of Blessing

1 Kings 3:16-4:34

USING YOUR BLESSINGS

IT MIGHT SOUND OBVIOUS, BUT NOW that you have that blessing from God that supplements your weaknesses, you have to actually use it. Many times, our weaknesses are so ingrained in us that we don't even know how or when to use that blessing when we need too. Or we still succumb to the lie that we aren't good at that, so why even try?

Think of it as a muscle that has never been trained or strengthened. God has given you the tools to exercise it and strengthen it through His blessing, but it won't be Schwarzenegger-level overnight. It will be uncomfortable and it will take time to perfect, but it will be possible because of God's blessing.

For example, if wisdom is what you asked God for, that doesn't mean you will immediately have a library of information stored in your head. Knowledge will still need to be sought out, but God's blessing will perhaps allow you to begin to understand what you research more easily. The right decision to make in a certain circumstance may seem clearer to you than it used to. The more you press into that blessing, the stronger it will become.

In 1 Kings 4, the author, speaking of Solomon's wisdom, says, "He spoke of trees, from the cedar that is in Lebanon to the hyssop that grows out of the wall. He spoke also of beasts, and of birds, and of reptiles, and of fish" (1 Kings 4:33). I highly doubt that when Solomon asked God for wisdom, God just downloaded an encyclopedia about lizards directly into his brain. Sure, it's possible, but I think it is more probable that His new God-given wisdom sparked a desire to research and understand, to build upon the gift that God had given him.

That is not to say that God's blessings are just weak little starter packs that really just depend on us. God's blessings are powerful and ready for instant use. Solomon was able to immediately put into practice using his newfound wisdom.

1 Kings 3 tells the most famous story of Solomon using his wisdom to rule. Two women came to him with a baby that they both claimed was theirs. They had both had their own baby but one had died, so the mother of the baby who died stole the baby of the other's and claimed that it was actually the other woman's baby that had died. They wanted Solomon to figure this out for them. What he initially proposes to solve this debate is absolutely brutal. He says, "Bring me a sword... Divide the living child in two, and give half to the one and half to the other" (1 Kings 3:24-25).

This does not seem wise to do. But he knew that, based on the reaction of the two women, he would be able to accurately decide whose baby it really was. And he was right. One woman was perfectly fine with this idea of cutting the child in two, while the other was horrified and offered to just let the other woman have the baby so that it didn't have to be killed. The one with compassion for the child was obviously the real mother, so he gave the baby to her.

This story wraps up in a very important statement that we cannot miss:

> And all Israel heard of the judgment that the king had rendered, and they stood in awe of the king, because they perceived that the wisdom of God was in him to do justice. (1 Kings 3:28)

The blessings that God gives us will do two things: they will glorify Him and fulfill the work that He wants to be done. When the Israelites heard of this wisdom the king had, they accredited it to God. They knew that it was *His* wisdom that was in Solomon. Sure, they were in "awe" of Solomon, but it was because they knew that God had blessed him. The wisdom Solomon used also established justice, something very close to the heart of God.

These are two very good filters to use when trying to establish ways in which to use your blessing. Ask yourself these questions in pretty much everything you do in marriage and fatherhood:

1. Does what I am about to do glorify God?
2. Does it accomplish what God wants to accomplish (or, in other words, does it line up with values of the Kingdom of God)?

When we try to manipulate the blessings that God has given us into glorifying ourselves or accomplishing something other than God has in mind, we are not properly using our gifts. God has given these blessings to us for a purpose.

Something that always fits nicely into these two filters is the act of blessing others out of the blessing that you have been given. This is an amazing way to spiritually lead your family. If God has gifted you with wisdom, give your family good guidance using that wisdom and knowledge. If God has given you peace, use it to calmly reassure and encourage your family when times get tough and be the solid support that they need. If God has given you strength and courage, make your family feel safe within that strength. Never withhold your blessings from them.

Solomon used his blessing to bless his people, and anyone else for that matter who sought it out. The Bible says, "And people of all nations came to hear the wisdom of Solomon, and from all the kings of the earth, who had heard of his wisdom" (1 Kings 3:34). It also says, "He...spoke 3,000 proverbs, and his songs were 1,005" (1 Kings 3:32). These examples of him not withholding his blessing from anyone are still evident today. The books of Proverbs, Song of Solomon, and Ecclesiastes were all written by him and that wisdom is still blessing us to this day.

Be generous with your blessing you have received just as God was generous in the gifting of it. Use it to bless your family.

I mentioned before that I was very sensitive when I was a child. That actually started to fade long before I went on the heavy dosage of anti-depressants. There had been some circumstances in my life as a child that caused me to begin, at an early age, to weed out of my life everything that made me seem weak. Emotions, especially sadness, and who I naturally was were some of the first to go.

I had a genuine desire as a child, as most people do, to be accepted and liked by everyone I came into contact with. Showing weakness, in my mind, would not make people like me, so I became whoever people wanted me to be. Depending on who I was around, I was a completely different person, tailored to each circumstance, giving me the best shot at being liked.

The truth was that as a kid, I had to figure out a lot of things on my own. At home, I wasn't engaged a lot by my parents. Now, don't get me wrong, I had, and have, great parents, but due to certain circumstances, ranging from my mom's illnesses to my dad's job, to name a couple, there were plenty of times that I had to go it alone.

I was left with this deep inner need for affirmation and acceptance and I went about that in many different ways. I tried to be the cool kid with the guys at school, getting into all sorts of trouble with them. I was a good listener and friend with the girls, eventually leading to being able to easily manipulate them into doing whatever I wanted. I was very mature and well-behaved with teachers, so that they thought highly of me. I was the "good" Christian kid at church. My life was a constant juggling act trying to portray whichever façade worked best for me in the moment, and as I got older, a lot of people got hurt from that.

The point I am trying to make, however, is the need at the bottom of all of that. There was a little boy that was in me during all of this trying to be liked. He was trying to find that affirmation and acceptance that he couldn't find at home a lot. That need wasn't bad, that little boy wasn't bad; just the ways that I was going about getting him that.

I see that little boy now in my two sons. I see him in my daughter. I even see him in my wife. These are all people that are within my kingdom that need love, affirmation, and acceptance from their dad and husband. And knowing what it is like to not have that as a kid, I am in a unique position to bless them with that. I know exactly what me as a little boy needed in his loneliest times. I am now able to bless them and give them that when they are at their loneliest and hopefully set them up better going forward than I was.

I don't withhold that blessing just because it was withheld from me. It actually empowers me more to give that blessing because I know where withholding it leads, and that is not somewhere I want the people in my family to go. I lead by blessing them.

Now, it might not sound like my wounding as a child is a blessing from God that I can now use to bless others. And in a way, you are right. What happened to me as a kid was not a blessing. But what came out of it was: compassion. God has blessed me with compassion for the lonely and sad, because as a kid, *I* was lonely and sad. And with that blessing, I can choose to be compassionate and loving to the people in my life so that they don't have to be lonely and sad. Oftentimes, our biggest blessings and the best parts of ourselves come out of the darkest times in our lives. It's God's way of resurrecting the dead parts of our lives and redeeming the terrible things that have happened to us. He uses them to bring life and blessing to others.

JESUS BLESSED OTHERS

Jesus was never withholding of His blessings to His people. He didn't have any weaknesses, but God nevertheless blessed Him, and He used those blessings to bless others.

A small, clear example of this can be found in Matthew 19:

> Then children were brought to him that he might lay his hands on them and pray. The disciples rebuked the people, but Jesus said, "Let the little children come to me and do not hinder them, for to such belongs the kingdom of heaven." And he laid his hands on them and went away. (Matthew 19:13-15)

This is a great picture of what Christ does for His Church to this day, and a good example of how we can bless our families. He blessed the ones that no one else wanted to. When the disciples tried to turn away the little children, Jesus corrected them and let them come. Who else would bless them if He wouldn't? Who else will bless us if He won't? And who else, besides Jesus, will bless your family if you won't? You are in a unique spot, as the spiritual leader of your family, to serve as a provider of blessing and the mediator of God's blessing.

This is also a good example of *how* you can bless your family. The laying on of hands was a way in the Bible, and still is in some cultures today, of showing blessing. Touch has a special way of showing the ones being touched that they are loved. I'm not saying that your children have to get on their knees and you bless them by touching their head, though that is certainly one option, but any loving touch can be used as a blessing. Hug your kids. Physically show affection for your wife without always having a sexual motive in mind. Be tasteful with it, but physically show affection for your family in public, to let them know that you are not ashamed to be with them. Physical blessing can be a great way to show your family that you love them.

It also said that the children came to Him so that He might pray for them as well. This is another great way to bless your family. Pray *for* them. Also, pray *with* them. Pray for them *while* you are with them. Tell God within their hearing what you are thankful for about them. Tell them directly what you are thankful for about them. Wives and kids need affirmation.

Constant silence and/or negative feedback will leave them feeling less than adequate. Families need to know what their dad loves about them.

Bless your family by spending actual time with them. Jesus could have prayed for the children from a distance, but He wanted them to come right to Him. He wanted them to be physically in His presence. Your family wants the same. Many times, men get caught up in the responsibility of providing physical resources and drop the ball when it comes to providing quality time and physical presence. Carve regular time out of your schedule to spend time with each member of your family, both all together and one-on-one.

Jesus also gave good gifts to His people, the Church. Gifts that would give the recipients value. One major example of this is His gift of grace. In doing so, the Bible says that we are now co-heirs with Christ. Talk about valuing His people! He has elevated us to the position of children of God! What gifts can you provide for your family members that will make them feel valued and loved?

One last way that Jesus blessed His people was through being a servant to them. He was God, but he lowered Himself to the station of a servant to show His love. He physically washed the feet of His disciples at one point, even though He was clearly the greatest leader among them. There is no better way to show leadership than serving. It may seem counterintuitive, but there isn't a person on earth who wouldn't follow a legitimate servant-leader. Bless your family by serving them, and not by lording your authority over them

(1 Peter 5:1-4). Show them that they are worth serving and being supported. The blessing and value that they will receive will be appreciated for their entire lives.

A good king never withholds blessing from the people he leads. Make sure to bring this sentiment into your marriage and relationships with your children. Love your family well by *showing* them you love them well.

EXPERIENCE

- Think back in your life to a time when blessing was withheld from you. This could be you as a child when you needed some affirmation from your father but he wasn't there to give it. Or maybe your mother wasn't the nurturer that you needed. Any past relationship where you were not adequately supported will work.
- If that little boy or man were standing in front of you today, what is a way that you could bless him now in order to give him what he needed then?
- Keep these methods in mind as you begin to bless the people in your family.
- Read Psalm 34.
- In what ways has God blessed you?
- Pray and thank God for these blessings.

CHAPTER 6
Spiritual Disciplines

1 Kings 6, 8, 9:25

GETTING TO KNOW GOD

THIS CHAPTER WILL ADDRESS THE MOST common practical conceptions most men probably think of when they think of spiritually leading their home. Those same conceptions are probably what men fear most, and are most insecure about, in regard to leading their families.

As the husband and father, it is your responsibility to guide your family in bringing them closer to God. The first step to this is growing closer to God yourself. A great vehicle for this is through implementing spiritual disciplines.

Now, I know the phrase "spiritual disciplines" can carry some negative connotations with some people, especially if you grew up in a religious culture where they were forced upon you, and if you did them wrong, you were shamed or told you were no good. But the actual point of spiritual disciplines is getting to know God better, so He can reveal Himself and His grace to us. They are never meant to make us feel bad about ourselves. Many people have attached legalism to them and made them hard rules that become a litmus test for our walk with God, but that shame and extra burden are put there by *people*, never by God.

God wants to have us know Him better. He wants to remove every obstacle between Him and us. That is why He sent His Son–so that we could be reconnected with Him. He has no intention of ever widening the gap between us or requiring us to do things to earn His love. Spiritual disciplines are not a way for us to earn His love. They are a way for us to *experience* His love.

A mentor of mine told me that spiritual disciplines are great for growing closer to God, but we should never become legalistic about them, because the moment we do, it would probably just be better not to do them at all. If we are legalistic about them, then they are something that we *have* to do, not something that we *want* to do. We shame ourselves and feel like God is mad at us when we forget or mess up, and we also become judgmental of others who do less than us or none at all. Neither of these bring us closer to God.

But as men, we will inevitably feel shame when we fall short of the standards that we place on ourselves. So, the best way to tackle this from the front end is set up a spiritual discipline schedule that is actually possible. Here is a list, though not exhaustive, of some common spiritual disciplines:

- God's Word: Reading, studying, memorizing, and meditating on the Bible.
- Prayer: Actual conversations with God, both scripted and unscripted.

- Silence: Taking time to just sit and listen to what God wants to say to you.
- Solitude: Being alone without any distractions to be with God.
- Fasting: Giving something up and using that time with God.
- Self-examination: Looking into your life and actions with regard to what is and isn't working; noticing how God is active in your life.
- Confession: Being honest with yourself, others, and God about your shortcomings and your need for grace.

Practicing spiritual disciplines is a marathon, not a sprint. They are meant to bring you closer to God and sanctify you, which takes time. Doing a bunch in a short period of time won't necessarily make it go faster. Also, you don't have to do every single one every single day. Some are better for daily use, like reading the Bible and praying, but fasting probably won't fit into your daily schedule. That might be something you do just once a year. There are no set rules to what you have to do, just make sure that it is something that you want[1] to do, you actually will do, and will bring you closer to God. If possible, it is better to set up these habits in your life *before* you enter into a marriage so that they will flow seamlessly into that marriage, and so that you can better include God in it from the start.

[1] By "want" here, I don't necessarily mean that you are super excited to do it every time (or any time, for that matter). Fasting isn't something that many people want to do ever. It is a discipline, like working out at the gym, and most people only go to the gym for how it will benefit them in their lives outside of the gym. What they actually want is to be strong and healthy. So even if a spiritual discipline isn't something you necessarily want to do, the end goal of having a closer relationship with God can be the motivating want that will inspire you to do it.

Set them up so that they fit into your schedule and set reminders so that the busyness of life won't get in the way. Phone reminders are extremely helpful, but this can be as simple as agreeing to pray whenever you brush your teeth in the morning, and picking up your toothbrush can be that reminder. Or every morning when you drive to work, when you would usually just be listening to music or a podcast, pray as you drive. Your seatbelt clicking into position could be your reminder. Look at your schedule and plan days throughout the year when you can fast and take some time of solitude. These heftier disciplines won't just happen on their own. After all, they are *disciplines*, just like going to the gym is. We have to make time for them and commit to following through.

The possibilities are endless. It would also be wise to sit down with a mentor or someone you trust and explain to them your plan and receive any input that they have for you. Their suggestions may surprise you.

I recently expressed to one of my mentors, James, that I wanted to quit smoking. I had also previously stated that I wanted to create a habit of some spiritual disciplines, but didn't know where to start. He connected some dots that I had not even thought of. He suggested that whenever I had the craving to smoke, I implement a simple spiritual discipline: a breath prayer. A breath prayer is exactly what it sounds like, a prayer you do while breathing intentionally. You inhale, pray some words, and then exhale, and pray some more words. The prayer was simple: "(Inhale) Breath of life. (Exhale) Christ in me." That was it. And I'd like to say that I was instantly cured of all nicotine addiction the moment I prayed my first breath prayer, but I wasn't, but it did help: it reminded me that Christ was right there with me in the midst of my struggles. It brought me closer to God.

Start thinking today of a plan of putting spiritual disciplines into your daily life. The plan will not create itself. You have to be very intentional about it. And as a man who wants to be the spiritual leader of your home, you have to be intentional about setting up a plan for your family and encouraging the people in your house to implement spiritual disciplines in your own life.

You are the leader and are responsible for this part of your family's life. Personal spiritual disciplines are great and very needed, but they are just that: personal. And marriage and fatherhood is not a single-person thing.

Ephesians 5, which we looked at in the beginning of this book, goes on to speak a bit more about how Christ loved the church:

> Husbands, love your wives, as Christ loved the church and gave himself up for her, that he might sanctify her, having cleansed her by the washing of water with the word, so that he might present the church to himself in splendor, without spot or wrinkle or any such thing, that she might be holy and without blemish. (Ephesians 5:25-27)

He (Jesus) cleansed her (the Church) by the washing of water with the Word. This is a beautiful picture of Jesus bringing the Word of God to His Church. And if we want to love our wives the way Christ loved the Church, we must do the same thing. I think it is safe to say that this should extend to our children as well. We are to aid God in sanctifying the people that He has entrusted to us. Sanctifying means "setting apart as holy" or "purifying." And sure, humans can only be truly sanctified and made clean by the blood of Jesus, but it is a lifelong journey and mission of making ourselves more like Jesus. We, above everyone else (except Jesus), are chosen to help with this for our families. Not just their pastors, teachers, or mentors. Us. The husbands and fathers. This is a huge responsibility that requires action. And, too often, men passively leave this important task to others.

How exactly do we do this? By instilling the same habits we have instilled in ourselves into the mechanics of our family. Pray together regularly. Read the Bible together regularly. Bedtime and meals are great times to do these with young children. Schedule family media fasts. Schedule time for your family to go into nature and just experience God there in silence and solitude. Go to church regularly at a church that *you* trust and can honestly trust with the teaching of your family. Worship together, both at church and in the home. Again, the possibilities are endless.

Begin by leading these things yourself, but as time goes on, encourage the others to step in and lead the prayers or readings. Give them some ownership and input, so they can begin to truly appreciate what is happening. Perhaps your wife has a great idea for a fast. Or your son has a spot in nature he wants to take the family. Listen to your family and what they have to offer. Leadership doesn't always mean that you have to have every idea, it just means that you have to go first.

The same guidelines apply: make a plan that you both want to do and can do, and don't shame yourself or your family members when it isn't done perfectly. Schedule them; make "family prayer time" a set thing that your family expects, and hopefully looks forward to. The goal here is to grow your family closer to God and get to know Him better, not heap on a bunch of strict rules that your family will come to hate, ending in resentment of you, God, or both.

In 1 Kings, we find many examples of Solomon setting up both personal spiritual disciplines, and spiritual disciplines for the people of his kingdom, all to bring glory to God and bring himself and his people closer to God.

Several instances of him making sacrifices are mentioned. Sacrifices were the way that followers of God atoned for their sins before Jesus died. It was the only way to reconnect yourself to Him in those days. So, the practice of this and the discipline of doing it regularly were very important. First, Solomon modeled this for his people. The Bible tells us in 1 Kings 3:3-4 that since Solomon loved the Lord, he would sacrifice a thousand animals at a time at a certain altar. This was before he built the temple, which would allow his entire kingdom to participate in regular offerings, but he was modeling it for them long before it was built. After he received his blessing of wisdom, he again made sacrifices and made a feast for all of his servants. This is another example of blessing his people out of the blessing that God had given him.

After the temple was built, he again made sacrifices, with everyone who was gathered there for the dedication. This was a massive affair. After a very heartfelt prayer thanking God and praying for his people, Solomon sacrificed 22,000 oxen and 120,000 sheep. That is a ton! He also threw a massive feast for all of Israel that lasted seven days. He went all out in the temple dedication, and instilled in his people the importance of what had been accomplished.

What exactly had been accomplished in the building of the temple? The answer to this question provides great insight into what we should be doing for our families spiritually.

David had always wanted to build a permanent temple—a permanent "house" that the Spirit of God would literally inhabit on earth. However, because of all the warfare during David's reign, he was unable to accomplish this desire (1 Kings 5:3). Conversely, during Solomon's reign there was peace on all sides of the kingdom. So Solomon decided to accomplish this task. He built a huge, beautiful temple full of the finest materials the world had to offer. And in doing so, he built a public structure that the people of his kingdom could come and be close to God and worship Him.

This is so important. Solomon recognized the fact that he was responsible for providing time and space for his people to become closer to God. He used absolutely massive amounts of resources to accomplish this, and in the end God had a place to dwell where His people could come to Him. Solomon was a huge factor in facilitating this relationship between God and the people he was leading.

Likewise, we must help facilitate that relationship between God and the members of our family. I'm not saying to build a shrine or a small chapel in your backyard where your family can go worship. The New Testament says that "your body is a temple of the Holy Spirit within you…" (1 Corinthians 6:19). Since Jesus' death on the cross paid for all of our sins, there is no longer a need to go to a specific physical location to be in God's presence. For those who believe, God has sent His Holy Spirit to dwell in us. Each follower of Christ is a temple. So, your job is to help facilitate those temples, which is literally each member of your family. Solomon went to grand extremes to remove the obstacles so that people had a place to worship God and sacrifice to Him. You can do the same thing by tending to the physical and spiritual bodies of your wife and kids.

The above passage from 1 Corinthians goes on to say, "You are not your own, for you were bought with a price. So glorify God in your body" (1 Corinthians 6:19b-20). Teach your wife and kids to glorify God with their bodies. Sexuality comes to our minds instantly when we think of this, and that is obviously true. We must teach our families to glorify God with their sexuality, but there are other ways to glorify God with our bodies. Teach them to take care of their bodies with good health. Our bodies are gifts from God. Teach them to use their bodies to worship God.

My kids love to sing, dance, and use motions to songs they learn in their classes at church. They will probably outgrow using motions to worship God eventually, but while they are young I encourage this in them and even sometimes join in. It is a hilariously fun way to engage with your kids in worship and teach them that worshiping God can be fun and silly, not always solemn, or what they may perceive as boring.

With your wife, respect her body and love her with yours. Never body-shame her or make her feel like she isn't enough physically or sexually. Encourage her in the ways that she wants to improve, but never make it feel like a requirement for your love and affection.

It is also important to note that when we get married, our bodies no longer belong to us alone. We become one flesh with our wives (Genesis 2:24). Paul puts it this way, in regard to sexuality:

> The husband should give to his wife her conjugal rights, and likewise the wife to her husband. For the wife does not have authority over her own body, but the husband does. Likewise the husband does not have authority over his own body, but the wife does. Do not deprive one another, except perhaps by agreement for a limited time, that you may devote yourselves to prayer; but then come together again, so that Satan may not tempt

you because of your lack of self-control.
(1 Corinthians 7:3-5)

Your bodies belong to each other and to God. So, come together sexually to glorify God. It is a beautiful picture of being one with your wife and with God. Never have sex to just glorify yourself or make yourself feel better. And never deprive your wife of sex, for whatever reason. Maybe you are mad at her, or maybe you are not happy with the way that she looks. This deprivation does not glorify God or her, but just brings shame and breeds resentment, driving a wedge in what God has brought together.

Paul also brings up an interesting idea in this passage in regard to fasting. He says that you may decide with your wife to fast from sex and devote yourselves to prayer. This is a good idea but there are four things to note here. First, make sure you are both on board with this idea. Come to this decision together. Second, it is only for a limited time. Come back together eventually. And third, do it to glorify God. Sex can glorify God, but also the fasting from sex can also glorify God if done in the right way. Lastly, this is not a command. You don't *have* to fast from sex. But it is an option if it appeals to both you and your wife.

Since we have established that our bodies and the bodies of our wives and kids are temples of the Holy Spirit, there is no longer a need to travel to a certain location to be with God like there was in the Old Testament. But that does not mean that attending a solid local church is not important. It is very important. Corporate worship and learning from educated teachers was not something that went away when the Holy Spirit started inhabiting people. It is your responsibility to find a good church that operates on sound doctrine and Biblical teaching, and partner with them in the spiritual education of your family. Being with other families in community is also an important benefit of attending a church. Find a church that you trust, and set up a habit of attending regularly with your family.

The Bible also teaches us the importance of financially supporting your church and the work that God is doing through it. It is your responsibility to decide between you and God what amount you are going to give. This is a very solid way to establish trust in God. Usually, our finances are the last thing we want to sacrifice, but be sure to set aside a portion of your money to go towards the work of God. Teach your kids to do the same. If they have allowances or jobs, teach them the importance of trusting God with their money. And be vulnerable; if you have fears around this, let them know so that they know that their fears are warranted. It can be scary to give your money away. But teach them that God promises to provide, and He blesses those who give.

Teach them the value of serving, as well. Solomon enlisted the labor of thousands of people in the construction of the temple. Teach your kids that the time and effort that they spend serving God and others will strengthen their faith and bring them closer to God.

Spiritual disciplines are how we grow closer to God. They

are a gift, not a list of rules. Share them with your family and grow together. As you do, you will grow closer to each other as well.

JESUS PRACTICED SPIRITUAL DISCIPLINES

Jesus was an absolute master of the spiritual disciplines. All throughout the Gospels we see Him prioritizing taking time to practice the disciplines of prayer, study, solitude, etc. But how did he use these to lead and love His people?

First, He was an amazing model of what it looks like to implement them into our lives. He went first. In the same way, you should go first in your family. And like I said, it will be easier if you start to implement them now, before you get into the craziness of family life.

Second, He taught others how to do it best. The best example of this is in Matthew 5-7, in His famous Sermon on the Mount. Take time to read through this, as it gives many great guidelines as to how to practice spiritual disciplines best. He gives many examples of what not to do, usually pointing to what the Pharisees were doing, and also how to do them well, like how and where to pray, and doing them solely for the glory of God, not to show everyone else how spiritual you are.

The point I am trying to make here is that He took actual time to instruct His followers on how to do it. He loved them enough to give them guidance on how it could be most beneficial to them. Do this with your family. Teach them how to do it and how not to do it. Correct them when they are off course, in love. Help them develop their own personal plans for spiritual discipline and formation. Wash them in the Word of God, and help them to reap the benefits of a closer walk with God.

Solomon was also a good example of how to teach the people he led. He wrote down and provided to the people his proverbs, songs, and experiences. Proverbs is full of great teaching. Song of Solomon is a love letter to a woman, speaking into their intimacy with each other and with God. And Ecclesiastes is his take on all the experiences he had throughout his life, and what he found beneficial and what he didn't. Sharing your experiences is paramount. A story from your own life in the midst of teaching and instructing your family will show them that you are vulnerable, trustworthy, and qualified to speak into their lives. All too often fathers try to come off as if they have everything figured out all the time. Wives and children can see through this façade and credit it to you as hypocrisy. Be honest with your family and teach them through the learning you have received through your experiences.

Jesus also gave His people purpose with a mission. Before He left the earth physically for a couple thousand years and counting, He famously gave His followers the Great Commission:

> And Jesus came and said to them, "All authority in heaven and on earth has been given to me. Go therefore and make disciples

of all nations, baptizing them in the name
of the Father and of the Son and of the
Holy Spirit, teaching them to observe all
that I have commanded you. And behold, I
am with you always, to the end of the age."
(Matthew 28:18-20)

This is an amazing example of leading and loving the
Church: giving them purpose and responsibility. Do this
with your family. Encourage your wife to engage in her own
ministry. Set up goals with your kids and instill in them a
passion to do the work of God. Yes, you are the leader, but
you should guide the ones you lead to their own purpose and
give them a responsibility for their own spirituality as well.
Proverbs 22:6 says, "Train up a child in the way he should
go; even when he is old he will not depart from it." How you
engage in the teaching and training of your children will have
life-long effects. Teach them to share their faith and what they
have learned with their friends. And never forget to support
them as they go about their purpose and missions in life. The
support of a loving husband and father can encourage them
to do great things. Do not quench their spirit. If they have
a passion for something that lines up with the heart of God,
even if you don't necessarily relate to it, encourage them in it.
God gives us all different callings. If we all did the same thing
the world would be a much more boring place. Do your best
to guide them, rejoice with them when they find that sense of

calling, and do whatever you can within your power to help them succeed.

EXPERIENCE

- Talk to a mentor or someone you look up to for spiritual guidance and ask them about their plan of spiritual disciplines.
- Ask them to speak into your plan. What do they think would best grow you closer to God?
- Think of one measurable step you can take in the week after speaking with them to begin a plan of spiritual discipline. Pick something and do it. Check in with your mentor on if you actually did it or not at the end of the week.

CHAPTER 7
Fallout of Failure

1 Kings 11

SOLOMON TURNS FROM THE LORD

YOU HAVE JUST MADE IT THROUGH THE MEAT of this book. You have become aware of what is expected of you as a husband and a father and been shown how to actually put it into practice. Admittedly, it is a lot. There is a ton that you, as the man of the house, are responsible for. So, what if you just feel like it is too much?

Well, it is going to take regular reminding and constant vigilance to keep your kingdom running smoothly. Even Solomon needed reminding of what was at stake and renewed motivation to keep it going.

Shortly after the temple was completed, God came and spoke to Solomon again. He reiterated the covenant that David spoke of: that Israel would not lack a man on the throne if that man followed God with "integrity of heart and uprightness" and doing everything God commanded him. Up to this point in his life, Solomon had been right on point. However, God still sees that it is necessary to remind him what exactly is at stake if he should fail.

But if you turn aside from following me, you or your children, and do not keep my commandments and my statutes that I have set before you, but go and serve other gods and worship them then I will cut off Israel from the land that I have given them, and the house that I have consecrated for my name I will cast out of my sight, and Israel will become a proverb and a byword among all peoples. And this house will become a heap of ruins. Everyone passing by it will be astonished and will hiss, and they will say, 'Why has the LORD done thus to this land and to this house?' Then they will say, 'Because they abandoned the LORD their God who brought their fathers out of the land of Egypt and laid hold on other gods and worshiped them and served them. Therefore the LORD has brought all this disaster on them.' (1 Kings 9:6-9)

Essentially, God is warning that if Solomon does not lead his kingdom well, it is going to fall apart. Literally become "a heap of ruins." Unfortunately for Solomon, he did not listen well enough.

Some years later, when Solomon was older, everything he had worked for fell apart. 1 Kings 11 tells us that he went against God's will of not marrying women who worshiped other gods. His desire for them led to disobedience. As God had warned him, they turned Solomon's heart away from Him and to their false gods and goddesses. He built places of worship for these false gods, allowing evil and idol worship into his kingdom. He spiritually led his kingdom astray.

God was not pleased:

> And the LORD was angry with Solomon, because his heart had turned away from the LORD, the God of Israel, who had appeared to him twice and had commanded him concerning this thing, that he should not go after other gods. But he did not keep what the LORD commanded. Therefore the LORD said to Solomon, "Since this has been your practice and you have not kept my covenant and my statutes that I have commanded you, I will surely tear the kingdom from you and will give it to your servant. Yet for the sake of David your father I will not do it in your days, but I will tear it out of the hand of your son. However, I will not tear away all the kingdom, but I will give one tribe to your son, for the sake of David my servant and for the sake of Jerusalem that I have chosen."
> (1 Kings 11:9-13)

The consequences of Solomon's bad choices were severe. The kingdom was to be torn away. It is so important to note exactly who the kingdom was to be torn away from, however. Solomon actually got to rule the kingdom until he died. It was his son who felt the harshest consequence.

Our choices, good or bad, do not just solely impact us. Our families suffer as well. If we fail to spiritually lead our families, and especially if we spiritually lead them astray, the consequences could affect your family for generations. The responsibility you carry is of extreme importance.

I am not saying that, if you lead your family well, there will be no problems. Jesus says, "In this world you will have trouble" (John 16:33). Despite our best efforts to control every circumstance of our lives, things will get bumpy sometimes. No one leaves home without scars. No one escapes childhood without significant wounds. It will happen. So, don't feel like a failure when, despite your best efforts, members of your family don't have a perfect life. Some things are out of your control. But they are not out of the control of Jesus. He says, in the same verse, "But take heart! I have overcome the world." There is always hope for those of us and our families who are struggling–just continue to point them to Jesus.

What I *am* saying, however, is that the failure to spiritually lead your family at all, or so poorly that you lead them in the wrong direction (away from God), will maximize your family's wounds and scars. Failure to protect them from outside influences will end in nothing but shame and disgrace, and the responsibility will lie with you. Worst of all, you will taint their view of marriage, and therefore their view of Christ and the Church, God, love, family, etc.

Let me end on a positive note, as the inverse of this hard truth is also true. If we lead our families well spiritually, the benefits and blessing will affect generations as well. David's success affected Solomon just as Solomon's failure affected his son, Rehoboam. God chose not to tear the kingdom from Solomon solely based on David's virtues. David's goodness even made the consequence for Rehoboam less than it could have been, by persuading God to not tear away the *entire* kingdom, just most of it. Let that excite you and motivate you to prioritize this part of leading your family. Bless them by putting in the hard work to successfully guide them towards God.

CONCLUSION

YOU ARE ENOUGH

YOU HAVE WHAT IT TAKES TO BE THE HEAD and
spiritual leader of your home. I know you do because God
graciously and generously gives us what we need. Being a man
is no easy task, and being a husband and father is even harder,
but God created us to lead. He placed us with our families to
help guide them and point them to Him.

You won't do it perfectly. No father or husband in history
has. But the grace of Jesus will cover you when you fall short.
Keep your head up and press on. Do not listen to the lies that
Satan will heap on you telling you that you can't do it or that
God must have made a mistake when picking you. God makes
no mistakes, and he chose you for a reason.

Lastly, when I say, "You are enough," I don't mean that
you *alone* are enough. You are *not* enough *on your own*. You
are only enough with God. So, don't puff yourself up with

pride and fall into the typical ways that men go about things: never asking for help, never admitting failure, never taking direction, etc. Do all of those things so that you can get better. God's word is there to guide you and His Spirit is living inside you to help you. And I've stressed it before and will stress it again: find other men to go alongside you! Strong, Godly men whom you trust and have your best in mind.

With God by your side, and Christ *in* you, you *are* strong and wise. There is no man better to lead your family spiritually than you.

So, let me leave you with these words. The same words that David said to Solomon before he handed the kingdom over to him:

> **Be strong and prove yourself a MAN.**
> **Follow God and listen to what He says so**
> **that your kingdom will prosper.**
> **Walk before Him in faithfulness and**
> **truth with all of your heart, soul,**
> **mind, and strength. If you do this, your**
> **kingdom will have a real MAN on the**
> **throne–a good husband and father–and**
> **no one will be able to take that from you.**
>
> (1 Kings 2:2-4, my paraphrase)

ACKNOWLEDGEMENTS

THANK YOU TO MY WONDERFUL WIFE, LEAH. Without you, I would not have had the motivation to figure any of this stuff out. Thank you for challenging me and helping me as I do my best to lead you and our kids. I love you.

Thank you to my kids: Jonah, Carter, and Eden. You all bring me so much joy and I am so proud of all of you. I am so fortunate that God has called me to be your dad. I love you all so much.

Thank you to my dad for believing in me, this project, and building into me all of these years. Thank you, mom, for loving me and always cheering me on.

Thank you to Flatirons for taking a risk on me with this project.

Thank you to Zack Weingartner for being my friend, but

ACKNOWLEDGEMENTS

also for being my editor. Your brilliance took this book up a notch. Thank you, Ben Foote, for also helping with the early phases of this material. You are a great friend and brother.

Thank you to Christian Cambier, Jason DeWitt, Alex Evans, Travis Hubbard, Stephen Mcbrayer, Matthew McKenzie, Stephen Moorman, Elliot Netzer, Dylan Palm-Trujillo, and Zane Sigafoos for letting me use you all as my guinea pigs with this material. You all are such great men, husbands, and future-husbands/fathers. Thanks for encouraging me and helping me to refine everything in this book.

And thanks to everyone who is reading this book. I hope that it helps in some way to inspire you to be the spiritual leader that your family is looking for, whether they know it or not.

ABOUT THE AUTHOR

JORDAN IS THE CONTENT & THEOLOGY PASTOR at Flatirons Community Church in Colorado. He has worked at Flatirons in some capacity since 2006, right after he graduated high school. He has worn many hats at Flatirons, from student ministry graphic designer to lighting director to creative director, and now to a pastor.

Jordan has been married to his wife, Leah Burgen, since 2010. They have three children: Jonah (6), Carter (5), and Eden (1).

Jordan is an avid Kentucky Wildcats fan. He also enjoys Hamburger Helper, hunting with his dog, Cooper, fantasy novels, cheap beer, and fine bourbon.